THREE PLAYS

ADVANCED READER COPY
PUBLICITY CONTACT: Norman Conquest
EMAIL: blackscat@outlook.com
PHONE: 616.469.0086
PUBLICATION DATE: Mar. 15, 2016

THREE PLAYS

THE TRIANGULATED DINER
THE DARK HYPOTENUSE
PRIMACY

D. HARLAN WILSON

Black Scat Books

PRAISE FOR THE WORK OF D. HARLAN WILSON

"Provocative entertainment."
—*Booklist*

"A bludgeoning celluloid rush of language and ideas served from an action-painter's bucket of fluorescent spatter."
—Alan Moore

"New bursts of stream-of-cyberconsciousness prose."
—*Library Journal*

"Wilson writes with the crazed precision of a futuristic war machine gone rogue."
—Lavie Tidhar

"Wilson invokes not a dialogue with readers but a bare-knuckle fistfight. Fascinating, horrifying, hilarious."
—*Publishers Weekly*

"Fast, smart, funny."
—Kim Stanley Robinson

"Pomo cybertheory never tasted so good!"
—*American Book Review*

"Utterly original."
—Barry N. Malzberg

"If reality is a crutch, Wilson has thrown it away."
—*Rain Taxi*

"A brilliant data screen of future memories."
—Arthur Kroker

"Wilson is both a ghost in the machine and a spanner in the works."
—*The Rumpus*

Three Plays
The Triangulated Diner • The Dark Hypotenuse • Primacy
Copyright © 2016 by D. Harlan Wilson
ISBN: 978-0-6926315-3-9

First Edition, March 2016

Acknowledgment is made to *The Strange Edge Magazine* where a flash version *The Dark Hypotenuse* was originally published.

Cover Photograph by Lodiza LePore

Cover Design by Norman Conquest

Illustration of Screaming Pope by Goodloe Byron
www.GoodloeByron.com

Black Scat Books
San Francisco, CA

www.BlackScatBooks.com

CONTENTS

For the Evolved. And the Jungle Depths.

"Life, as we find it, is too hard for us; it brings us too many pains, disappointments and impossible tasks. In order to bear it we cannot dispense with palliative measures . . . There are perhaps three such measures: powerful deflections, which cause us to make light of our misery; substitutive satisfactions, which diminish it; and intoxicating substances, which make us insensible to it."

—Sigmund Freud, *Civilizaiton and Its Discontents*

"Aggression unopposed becomes a contagious disease."

—Jimmy Carter, 11 January 1980 Speech

THE TRIANGULATED DINER

CHARACTERS

Roarke
The Waitress
Big Rita
The Psychologist
Invisible Men
The Therapist
The Associates
A Pornstar
A Gunman
Diners
Shoppers
Hotel Guests

SCHIZE

In this one-act schematism, a middle-aged man with a hangover goes to a diner.

The diner is a kind of culinary museum distinguished by appliances, wallpaper, décor and bric-a-brac from another era or dimension. The geometry of the diner belongs somewhere else, too, ceiling and walls forming a deranged rhombus.

The diner occupies the basement floor of an evacuated industrial elevator shaft. Several stories above it is an open-air mall. A matrix of wide copper pipes stretches from one balcony to another. Echoes of mall traffic intermingle with a drizzle of champagne music.

Outside the elevator door is a hotel lobby. The blood red carpet compliments the bright Venetian colors of the registration counters, baroque furniture, Tiffany chandeliers, and liquor bottles aligned above the bar. A blue waterfall pours from a long slit in the wall into a stone decanter.

We can't actually see the mall or the hotel lobby. There are two super-screens that represent each interzone, mainly in the form of foot traffic. The hotel superscreen (PORTSCREEN) is affixed to the LEFT

WALL; the mall superscreen (ÜBERSCREEN) hangs above the stage in the HEAVENS of the theater.

There is also a superscreen (GOODSCREEN) on the RIGHT WALL. Colorful amoebas of light flow across it in slowtime. When the amoebas collide, one assimilates the other, like protoplasm. Sometimes they ricochet, lobes groping for stability.

The POV of the GOODSCREEN remains fixed. The POVs of the PORTSCREEN and ÜBERSCREEN have the ability to zoom in and out on any aspect of their respective interzones from any angle.

Center stage is a long, angled counter with cushioned barstools. Upstage is a squeaking swing-door that leads to the kitchen and a slot where the cooks put food to be served. Stage left and right, people eat and talk quietly in booths. No matter what happens in the diner, they eat and talk quietly throughout the entire play, oblivious to the actions of the central characters.

HAJIME

[Roarke enters, stage right, and steps towards a barstool. Screaming, Big Rita enters, stage left, and tries to derail him with a forearm. Roarke sidesteps her and throws an elbow into the nape of her skull. She goes down hard.]

ROARKE: *Siparium.*

[He slumps into a bar stool and stares at the audience with his mouth half open.]

ROARKE: Mimosa!

[A waitress enters from the kitchen and stands behind the counter *with pen and paper at the ready.*]

ROARKE [*to the audience*]: Mimosa! Mimosa, goddamn it!

WAITRESS: Good morning, Roarke.

ROARKE [*to the waitress*]: You don't know my name.

WAITRESS: I know enough.

ROARKE [*retching*]: You don't know my name.

WAITRESS: I'm sorry, Roarke.

ROARKE: Stop calling me my name!

WAITRESS [*short pause*]: So.

ROARKE: Right.

WAITRESS [*long pause*]: So.

ROARKE: Orange juice and champagne in a glass. Mimosa!

WAITRESS: The diner doesn't serve mimosas. There are no mimosas at the diner.

ROARKE [*pounding the counter*]: That's a goddamn lie!

WAITRESS [*pensively*]: I don't want to sleep with you. I don't find you attractive. It's clear that your subjective perception of yourself is that you are an attractive man. But I am part of the objective world. *Le monde objectif.*

[*Roarke gets up and exits, stage right. He comes back and sits down again on the bar stool, fingering the counter nervously.*]

ROARKE: Coffee and water. No food.

[*The waitress exits. Big Rita screams from the floor. She tries to get up but Roarke stomps on her head, knocking her cold.*]

[*The waitress returns from the kitchen with a small glass of water and a cup of coffee.*]

ROARKE [*sipping the coffee*]: Disgusting. This coffee tastes like mud! [*He sips the coffee again.*] It's all right, I guess.

WAITRESS: I just made a fresh pot.

ROARKE: That's a goddamn lie.

WAITRESS: You're right. The pot isn't fresh.

ROARKE: I knew it.

WAITRESS: Knowledge isn't everything.

ROARKE: Knowledge isn't anything.

WAITRESS: You're right.

ROARKE: What's that smell?

WAITRESS [*sniffing*]: I don't smell anything out of line. I assume the smell you detect is an anomaly within the empire of your sensorium. *Le monde objectif* detects nothing but constancy and order. Occasionally it detects body odor.

ROARKE: I put on deodorant yesterday morning. Prescription strength! I still smell something bad.

WAITRESS [*making an obscene gesture*]: This isn't consensual. Just so you know.

[*Roarke and the waitress freeze like mimes. This happens every time the psychologist speaks.*]

PSYCHOLOGIST [*offstage, quoting Darwin*]: "There are many other structures and instincts which must have been developed through sexual selection—such as the weapons of offense and the means of defense of the males for fighting with and driving away their rivals—their courage and pugnacity—their various ornaments—their contrivances for producing vocal or instrumental music—and their glands for emitting odors, most of these latter structures serving only to allure or excite the female."

[*The lights in the theater flicker ominously during the psychologist's soliloquy, which is set to the hallucinogenic sound of a theremin that lends a B-Movie quality to the scene. When the psychologist finishes, the lights turn off as the notes of the theremin slink through the darkness like ethereal caterpillars.*]

[*Silence.*]

[*Lights. An avalanche of violence rolls across the stage—a battle royal between men dressed like James Whale's Invisible Man, with bandaged heads, mirrored goggles, fedoras, frock coats . . . None of them carry weapons, but the battle is nonetheless cruel and gruesome, blood spewing from unseen wounds.*]

[*The last man standing bows, then removes his clothes and stomps offstage, naked and invisible. The curtain, as if by accident, falls like a slammed window.*]

[*Rancorous industrial machinery accompanies the clumsy reopening of the curtain, which raises in fits and starts. The waitress is gone. Still frozen, Roarke stares at a giant blender on the counter beside him. Its jade-green frame stretches up and curls sharply into a long chrome cup; it looks like a crouched, mechanical pelican waiting to strike a herring.*]

ROARKE [*unfreezing*]: I don't understand this blender.

[*A laff track ignites offstage. With a jerk, Roarke stands and glares in the direction of the laff track until it peters out and falls silent. We never hear it again.*]

[*Roarke sits and the waitress exits the kitchen.*]

ROARKE [*sniffing*]: I love the smell of mimosas. They smell good.

WAITRESS: The diner doesn't serve mimosas. Gesturing towards them with hollow rhetoric won't conjure them to life.

ROARKE: Can I have a chocolate malt?

WAITRESS: I have never made a bad chocolate malt.

ROARKE: I don't understand this blender.

WAITRESS: It's a blender.

ROARKE [*short pause*]: Can I have a chocolate malt?

WAITRESS [*long pause*]: I have never made a bad chocolate malt.

ROARKE [*short pause*]: Can I have another cup of coffee?

WAITRESS: One drink at a time. That's a statute for existence.

ROARKE: I don't have a drink.

WAITRESS: You had a drink. One drink at a time.

ROARKE: It's not possible to drink more than one drink at a time. Even if you're holding two drinks—one in each hand. You can't take two sips at a time. The human mouth isn't big enough. Hence your so-called statute for existence is a default condition. It's no more a statute than a fallen cloud.

WAITRESS: That's called fog.

ROARKE: I know what fog is.

WAITRESS: Fog is the residue of Dawn's nightmares.

ROARKE [*short pause*]: You can't drink two drinks at a time.

WAITRESS: You can tilt your head backwards, open your mouth, and carefully pour two sips from two separate drinks into your gullet. Hence you will achieve simultaneity—which is to say, two drinks at a time.

ROARKE: Are you crazy? Nobody does that.

WAITRESS: Right now, somewhere on this planet, somebody is doing just that. Among other things.

ROARKE [*irritably*]: Why don't you ever laugh? Why are you so goddamn serious?

WAITRESS: I'm not that serious. As for laughter—once you laugh with angels, you need not laugh again.

ROARKE [*acidly*]: Your face is a mask of indifference and nonbeing. It's hysterical and makes me laugh. There's nothing funnier than people who take themselves seriously.

WAITRESS: On the contrary, there's nothing more serious than people who tell bad jokes.

ROARKE: Are you calling me a joke-teller? I don't tell "jokes," bad or otherwise. I suppose there are no good jokes. I've never heard a good joke. They're too performative. All the while you know they hinge on a final oratorical strike that will reliably fail to deliver any form of "joy" or "delight." When the joke-telling is done, I always laugh, but my laughter is as performative as the weird enactment of the joke itself.

WAITRESS: Angels tell the best jokes. Demons lack a sense of humor.

ROARKE: Are you calling me a demon who lacks a sense of humor? Or are you in some way, by deflection and sleight of words, calling me a songbird? I am not a songbird.

[*Squawking, Big Rita springs to her feet and blitzes Roarke. He ducks aside, trips her. She falls and rolls into a curtain that appears to swallow her.*]

[*Cue theremin . . .*]

PSYCHOLOGIST [*offstage, quoting Deleuze and Guattari*]: "Perhaps the basic idea is this: the unconscious is 'productive.' To say that it produces means that we must cease to treat it, as we have up till now, as a kind of theater in which a very special drama, the drama of Oedipus, is enacted. We believe that the unconscious is not a theater, but a factory."

ROARKE [*to the audience*]: I can see the ether.

WAITRESS [*polishing the blender*]: Nonetheless I will not sleep with you. Don't ask me again. I am not a lady. But I am more than a woman.

[*Lights fade.*]

[*PORTSCREEN brightens. ZOOM to an alcove of elevators in the hotel lobby. One elevator dings and the doors slide open. A bellhop pokes out his head and looks both ways, as if preparing to cross a busy street. His hat falls off. He bends over to pick it up . . . and is trampled by the occupants of the elevator standing behind him. VIOLENT TRACKING SHOT as they storm the hotel bar and antagonize the bartenders and cocktail servers. JUMP CUT to a WIDE SHOT of the elevator where the bellhop lies unconscious, face-down, sticking halfway out of the compartment. Unable to close, the doors repeatedly slide together into his ribcage.*]

[*Lights.*]

[*Roarke stands downstage with a contorted expression that belongs to a man in a silent film. He peers upwards, devoutly, helplessly, as if uncaging a thousand birds of prayer.*]

[*Lights fade.*]

[*ÜBERSCREEN brightens. CLOSE ON a man who has climbed onto one of the pipelines that runs between the mall's balconies. This is Roarke's therapist. He keeps his office in the mall between Banana*

Republic and Yankee Candle. The therapist wears a white turtleneck. Two men in black turtlenecks follow him, crawling ungracefully across the pipeline. Roarke wonders if they are chasing him and gesticulates at his therapist, trying to get his attention.]

[*It becomes clear that the men in turtlenecks aren't chasing the therapist. Together they reach the other side of the pipeline and descend a makeshift fire escape that zigzags all the way down to the kitchen of the diner. CAMERA FOLLOWS their descent.*]

[*Lights.*]

[*From the kitchen: the clanking of pots and pans, the singe of hot grease, loud cursing in Spanish, possibly Portuguese . . . The therapist and his companions exit the kitchen and stride across the stage towards Roarke, adjusting their turtlenecks. Roarke spins on the barstool and turns to them expectantly. The waitress puts the mop aside, smooths out her uniform and pushes her breasts together.*]

WAITRESS: What can I offer you gentlemen? A round of mimosas on the house? I'll sleep with you, if you like. Shall I take off my clothes and show you my nudity?

ROARKE: Hey!

THERAPIST: Calm down, Mr. Roarke. Outbursts of that nature belong to adolescent boys and frustrated proletariats.

WAITRESS: I agree.

ROARKE [*standing defiantly*]: Are you calling me a songbird? Why is everybody calling me a songbird? [*He makes a gesture indicating what one does when one snatches a bird from the air and crushes it in one's hand.*] And it's only Roarke. There's no mister.

You know my name.

THERAPIST: I know your name. My deepest apologies.

WAITRESS [*removing her clothes*]: I'll lie down on the counter and you can do what you like to my body. Shall I raise my legs in the air and make them into a V-shape? I will articulate the V in such a way that you can see my shantytown.

ROARKE: Stop that!

THERAPIST: There's no need for V-shapes, my dear. Thank you. Coffee will be fine. Coffee and eggs. Black coffee. Three eggs, sunnyside down. And bacon. Eight strips, extra crispy. Burnt, if you please. Sausage gravy and biscuits as well. Make that one biscuit. Are dumplings on the menu? One dumpling please. Thank you.

[*Distressed, the waitress clutches her uniform at the chest and hurries offstage, feeling violated.*]

ROARKE: I'm not entirely certain I know what a dumpling is.

THERAPIST: I have no idea what a dumpling is. And I don't want to know. But they taste good, and it's fun to say "dumpling." Only a monster would fail to enjoy, if not revel in, the vocalization of such a word.

ROARKE [*straight-faced*]: Dumpling.

THERAPIST: Precisely.

PSYCHOLOGIST [*offstage, sans theremin, misquoting Freud*]: "Do you remember that I won an Academy Award? When I accepted it at the Oscars, I thanked God and then called myself my own hero. This is the nature of the contemporary celebrity. There are no more taboos—only totems. One totem. The animal of the Self. The animus of Destruction."

ROARKE [*to the therapist*]: Isn't that two totems?

THERAPIST [*pensively*]: Two totems.

ROARKE [*peering offstage*]: Who the hell is out there? What the hell is he talking about?

THERAPIST: I didn't say anything.

[*Long silence.*]

ROARKE [*sitting down*]: Who are these joysticks? [*He motions at the therapist's companions.*]

THERAPIST: My associates.

ROARKE: Your associates?

THERAPIST: My associates.

ROARKE: Why do you need associates? Don't you have a secretary? Isn't that enough?

THERAPIST: I am my own secretary. You know this very well.

ROARKE: What do they make? I mean, how much money do you pay the associates to be your associates?

THERAPIST: They work for free. But I have promised each of

them a letter of recommendation, and they are getting good experience vis-à-vis their many associative duties and goings-on.

ROARKE: Vis-à-vis? Goings-on? You sound like an old woman who lives in an attic. You look like one too.

THERAPIST: Apropos. You missed your appointment last month. Here is the bill for the hotel room.

[*The therapist clicks his fingers and one of his associates hands Roarke a slip of paper. Roarke studies it.*]

ROARKE [*sickened*]: Hotel? I didn't stay in any hotel. I certainly didn't stay in a hotel for EIGHT HUNDRED AND SEVENTY-FIVE DOLLARS AND TWENTY-FOUR CENTS! Do I look like a person who stays in a hotel for EIGHT HUNDRED AND SEVENTY-FIVE DOLLARS AND TWENTY-FOUR CENTS? Do I look like a person who stays in a hotel for any price?

THERAPIST: Everybody stays in hotels, Mr. Roarke. It's part and parcel of the human condition. It's essential, in fact.

ROARKE: That's classist. Proles don't stay in hotels. They never leave their sheds except to use the outhouse and steal groceries. And it's Roarke. Only Roarke.

THERAPIST: Yes. Of course. My sympathy.

ROARKE: That doesn't make any goddamn sense. Your failure to articulate my signature doesn't mitigate the giving of sympathy.

THERAPIST: Is empathy what you're after?

ROARKE: Empathy is better than sympathy. But empathy is a

myth. Nobody can feel what somebody else feels. One can only feel what one feels. Empathy is an illusion. An illusory projection of sympathy for the self.

THERAPIST [*consulting the associates, then casting a flyhook glance at Roarke*]: Hotels are the lost wombs of the Mother. Nobody can have them, but everybody wants them. And everybody certainly dwells in them from time to time.

ROARKE [*confounded*]: What the hell is wrong with you? A hotel can serve as the Father as much as the Mother. Consider, if nothing else, how a hotel reaches for the vulva of the sky like the Phallus.

THERAPIST: That's a rudimentary understanding of what constitutes the Phallus. The Phallus is not merely a mimetic illustration of an erect penis. In fact, the Phallus only concerns the penis in terms of the penis's imaginary and symbolic functions. Otherwise the penis is an utter superfluity.

[*A string on the theremin snaps, producing a sonic whine. All of the characters cover their ears and peer offstage. Roarke stamps his foot and grunts.*]

ROARKE: Hey! Are you calling my penis a—?

THERAPIST: We are going to leave now. It is very nice to see you. Please take care of that bill at once. [*He glances fearfully into the hotel lobby.*] I expect to see you on Tuesday in my office. Please call Janet to confirm. Thank you in advance.

ROARKE: That's goddamn insane. You only just got here! What about your breakfast? I'm not paying for your breakfast!

[*The therapist and his associates exit the stage and proceed across the hotel lobby, taking delicate steps, as if the floor is an eggshell that might break . . . Roarke watches them go with a heavy heart, then spins on the barstool and hunches over the counter, reviewing the particulars of the hotel bill.*]

[*A spotlight falls on the curtain, stage left. Something rustles behind it. Big Rita leaps from the curtain and charges Roarke on all fours. Her scream is abnormal, unholy. It sounds like it belongs in another dimension.*]

[*Just as she is about to overtake Roarke, she pushes herself onto her hind legs and throws out her arms like a stuffed bird of prey.*]

[*At the moment of impact, Roarke slides off the barstool onto his knees, leans back and punches Big Rita in the groin as she clamors by. Clutching herself, she collapses and once again rolls away, this time stage right. There is a disturbance in the GOODSCREEN. The amoebas experience a visually grotesque frenzy as Big Rita's scream hits a crescendo . . . and fades into silence. When the scream is gone, the amoebas return to normal.*]

ROARKE [*to the audience*]: Once you leave the diner—there is no diner. I'm gonna miss that old bitch. [*He stands.*] Waitress! Waitress! Waitress! Waitress! Waitress! Waitress!

[*The waitress brings the therapist's order from the kitchen on a large platter. She puts the coffee on the counter first, then a plate of eggs and bacon, a plate of biscuits, a bowl of sausage gravy, and finally a large glass jar that, at first glance, looks like it contains an unborn baby.*]

ROARKE [*staggering backwards*]: What is that! What is it!

WAITRESS: A dumpling.

ROARKE: Oh.

[*The waitress places a large slip of paper beside the meal.*]

ROARKE: What is that?

WAITRESS: The bill.

[*Roarke takes the bill from the counter and steps downstage. As he reads the bill, his expression becomes increasingly traumatized. He goes back to the counter, retrieves the hotel bill his therapist gave him, and steps back downstage, examining the two bills at once.*]

ROARKE: EIGHT HUNDRED AND SEVENTY-FIVE DOLLARS AND TWENTY-FOUR CENTS. Both bills are EIGHT HUNDRED AND SEVENTY-FIVE DOLLARS AND TWENTY-FOUR CENTS! [*He steps backwards until he bumps into a barstool and flops onto it.*] There must be a connection. A connection between the hotel and the diner. And everything. Everything is connected. We're all connected to one another, and there's meaning everywhere, and everything means the same thing, and that's a good thing. The proof is in the billing. In the end, life is worth the egregious price of admission.

WAITRESS [*leaning over the counter and snatching the bill for the meal from his hand*]: I gave you the wrong bill. That's my dry cleaning bill. Please forgive me. I keep all the bills—my own bills and my customers' bills. I keep them in my dirty skirt. Here. That's your bill.

ROARKE: I didn't order this food! [*He reads the new bill.*] Well, that's more reasonable, at least. [*Eyeballing the waitress.*] But the fact remains that your dry cleaning bill is the exact same as my therapist's hotel bill. Is this a goddamn joke? Are you in cahoots with my therapist? Is everybody in cahoots with my therapist?

WAITRESS: Cahoots is a silly word. A silly word for a silly man. Enjoy your breakfast.

ROARKE: That's not my breakfast! Mimosa!

WAITRESS: I wouldn't sleep with you if you were the last baboon on earth. And I am extremely attracted to baboons. The slope of their muzzles. Their heavy jaws and canine teeth. Their static electric manes . . . I don't care about their bodies. Hairy legs, hairy arms and hairy genitals are all I require.

ROARKE: Are you calling me a monkey now?

WAITRESS: No. The last thing I'd call you is a monkey. Uncaged, monkeys are capable and free. You look like the sort of person who would throw a pornstar off of a roof.

ROARKE: What? I've never thrown a pornstar off of a roof! Why would I throw a pornstar off of a roof? What kind of thing is that to say?

[*Roarke and the waitress freeze like mimes. Lights dim and PORTSCREEN brightens. Prior to this scene, there has been little action in the hotel beyond guests quietly checking in and out of their rooms. Now we see the therapist. He's talking to the concierge, who stands behind a lectern. The associates flank the therapist like bodyguards. SLOW ZOOM on the exchange. We can't hear what's being said, but the concierge becomes more and more agitated, hammering the lectern with a fist. The associates accost the concierge; grabbing his shoulders, they shake him up and down and push him back and* forth. CAMERA STOPS. *The therapist steps behind himself, reaches into his jacket and unsheathes two pistols. Spreading his arms, he aims the pistols at his associates . . . and fires. Realtime skids into slowtime and CAMERA ZOOMS IN & SWINGS AROUND. The bullets enter the heads of the associates. CAMERA SWITCHES TO REVERSE ANGLE as the bullets explode out the other end, shards of bloody skull ejecting from the exit wounds. As if in response to the carnage, the associates' turtlenecks unravel and flap like bandanas in the wind before slowtime returns to realtime and their bodies crumple to the floor.*]

[*CAMERA PULLS OUT as the therapist paces backwards across the lobby, pointing the guns at the shell-shocked, blood-spattered concierge.*]

[*The therapist shoots the concierge in the face and his head explodes like a piñata.*]

[*He continues to pace backwards. Before disappearing offscreen, the therapist abducts a pornstar clinging to a nearby pillar. She wears heavy mascara, fake eyelashes, bouncy hair extensions, a tight half-shirt, skinny jeans and high heels. CAMERA FOLLOWS as he ushers her into a nearby stairwell by the arm and drags her up multiple flights, pausing to berate her. A cacophony of heavy metal music floods the theater during the ascent and surges during the therapist's tirades. Realtime slips into fasttime and slowtime with no apparent purpose or design. At the top of the stairway, the therapist kicks open a door and pushes the pornstar into the sunlight. The music is supplanted by a steady, earsplitting batshriek. The pornstar covers her eyes and staggers forward, trying to gain her bearings. CLUMSY, DISORIENTING CAMERAWORK. Shots of the sky, the rooftop, antennas and buildings across the street . . . SOLARIZED JUMP-CUT to the blurry POV OF THE PORNSTAR. Hysterical, she cries out and gasps for air . . . In time, her breath gets steadier and her vision becomes crisper, clearer. The sky is the color of amber, and her gaze locks onto a bald eagle that glides overhead in a clumsy, dizzying circle.*]

PORNSTAR: Father?

[*Screaming like Big Rita, the pornstar's POV garbles as she is lifted overhead by somebody behind her, carried to the edge of the roof and thrown off. A sidewalk speeds into her POV and the pornstar's scream is punctuated by a crunch, a splat, and darkness.*]

[*All superscreens switch off and the theater goes completely dark. Tentative notes escape the theremin.*]

PSYCHOLOGIST [*offstage, quoting the psychotic Dr. Schreber*]: I existed frequently without a stomach. Of other internal organs, I will only mention the *gullet* and the *intestines*, which were torn or vanished repeatedly, further the *pharynx*, which I partly ate up several times, finally the *seminal cord*, against which very painful miracles were directed, with the particular purpose of suppressing the sensation of voluptuousness arising in my body.

[*PORTSCREEN flickers on. LONG SHOT of a monochrome urban skyline distinguished by the smokestacks of factories and the steeples of churches. CAMERA RETREATS backwards across the roof, down the stairwell and into the hotel lobby, where a horde of detectives lazily frisk guests. Once we settle into a WIDE SHOT that includes the hotel bar, the other superscreens come back on along with the stage lights. Shortly thereafter, Roarke and the waitress unfreeze.*]

ROARKE [*indifferent*]: I didn't do that.

WAITRESS: You didn't do what?

ROARKE [*epiphanic*]: I knew it!

WAITRESS: You knew what?

ROARKE [*bedeviled*]: I don't know.

WAITRESS: I know . . . But you did in fact do that.

ROARKE: I'm leaving.

[*Roarke gets up and marches away, stage right. The waitress inspects the food she brought out. She eats a strip of bacon, dips a biscuit in the sausage gravy and takes a bite. Roarke returns. He's carrying a hairy object.*]

ROARKE [*angrily*]: I found this prop in the dirt. [*He throws it on the counter.*]

WAITRESS: What is it?

ROARKE: A wig, I think. It's not moving. It could be anything. It could be a beard. It could be the beard of God. Or a starfish. Are starfishes hairy?

WAITRESS: Starfish.

ROARKE: Starfishes is a acceptable plurality. So is fishes if you're talking about different species of fishes. If you're only talking about one species, though, and there's a bunch of them in a pot, the plural form is fish. Like, if I had a pot of white bass, it would be fish, but if I had a pot of white bass, sturgeon, perch, walleye and sheepshead, it would be fishes. I bet you didn't know that. Do you know anything?

WAITRESS: Sheephead. And there's only one species of starfish. They're all echinoderms.

ROARKE: Are you living on this planet? There's all kinds of different species of starfishes. Also, sheephead and sheepshead are both acceptable as plural and singular forms.

[*Roarke and the waitress stare at the object.*]

WAITRESS: I don't think that thing belongs to God.

ROARKE: What about the President of the United States? Do you think it belongs to him? Did you know that the President of the United States installed himself in the White House solely for the purpose of alien exploration? He's channeling all of the funds into alien research. People are starving. Businesses are collapsing. China's military could mop the floor with us. All because he wants to see a bug-eyed monster.

WAITRESS: That's preposterous.

ROARKE: He admitted it on national television! He bragged about it, even, telling everybody how stupid they were for, firstly, electing him, and secondly, for not believing in alien life. He's in the Oval Office right now using our most expensive orbital satellites to scrutinize deep space. He doesn't care about getting re-elected. He made a bet with his mother: if he won the Presidency, he would find extraterrestrials in the span of four years. If he loses the bet, he has to build his mother a modest seaside resort in Portofino where she can bring all of her friends to play bridge and drink Bellinis. She's Italian. Don't you watch the television? Do you know that most living people don't believe in life beyond earth? All they believe is their reflection in the mirror.

WAITRESS: That's ridiculous.

ROARKE: You probably don't know that the First Lady had her foot amputated either.

WAITRESS: That's outrageous.

ROARKE: I'm serious. I'm always serious. The First Lady, the President's wife, had her foot amputated. She said she stepped on a jellyfish somewhere on the coast of Martha's Vineyard and got an infection, but the President is of course convinced that the Bad Foot was the product of covert earthbound aliens who don't want him to find out where they came from. It's a conspiracy, he thinks. A conspiracy relegated, for the time being, to his wife's foot.

WAITRESS: What are you talking about?

ROARKE: I'm talking about reality. The reality of our predicament. The President believes in Extraterrestrial Biological Entities. So do I. But I also believe in myself. Ideology is out of control. Anything could happen. Anybody could die.

WAITRESS [*walking away*]: Your food is getting cold. There are no refunds. *Huis clos.*

ROARKE: I'm not paying for this! This isn't mine!

[*The waitress goes into the kitchen. Distraught, Roarke plays with the food, pouring sausage gravy onto the eggs and pushing them around the plate with a fork.*]

[*A man comes out of the kitchen and positions himself beside Roarke. He is dashingly handsome and wears a double-breasted suit. His face may or may not be a mask. In his arms, he cradles an Uzi like a pet. Roarke either doesn't notice him or chooses not to acknowledge him.*]

GUNMAN [*cocks the handle of the Uzi*]: I used to wrestle iguanas in the desert. That was at least three lifetimes ago. Now I just shoot everything that moves until the last man standing is myself. Meaningless violence is the only agency.

[*The gunman fires indiscriminately into the crowd, into the hotel, into the mall, maneuvering the Uzi up and down as he turns in circles like a mannequin on autopilot. The Uzi is maddeningly loud. Bullets whiz and whistle in every direction. Mall-goers and hotel guests yell and run for cover as they are injured, killed. Whenever a bullet strikes somebody on a superscreen, the wound explodes like a squib and spurts bright red blood. Nobody in he audience of the theater gets hit.*]

[*The gunman continues to fire until he runs out of bullets. It becomes clear that, above all, he wants Roarke's attention. Roarke doesn't flinch, and not once does he so much as glance at the gunman. Nor do the other occupants of the diner despite several of them being shot to death.*]

[*When the clip is empty, the gunman continues to pull the trigger, clicking it like a metronome. Indignant, he drops the gun onto the stage and kicks it aside.*]

GUNMAN [*deadpan*]: It's saddening to die in a hail of bullets. I heard that on the radio.

[*Melancholy, the gunman returns to the kitchen.*]

[*Passionate moans emanate from backstage. Roarke's ears prick up. He gets off the barstool and goes to the end of the counter, stretching out his neck, listening . . . The moans grow louder and more rhythmic. A table or chair squeaks.*]

ROARKE: Hey! Is everybody all right in there? What's going on in there?

[*An orgasmic cry stops him from going backstage. Depressed, he returns to the barstool and slumps onto it with a heavy head.*]

[*The waitress steps out of the kitchen. Her uniform is torn and her hair is disheveled. She tries to put herself back together as she surveys the diner.*]

WAITRESS [*quoting Jacques Lacan*]: "Everything that is written stems from the fact that it will forever be impossible to write, as such, the sexual relationship. *La relation sexuelle ne peut pas s'écrire.*"

[*Roarke glares at the waitress as she proceeds to clean the diner at a rapid pace, dragging dead bodies offstage, sweeping and mopping the floor, tidying up tables and even cashing out several diners. During this interval, the hotel and the mall are sanitized by a team of janitors as CAMERA FOLLOWS an avalanche of detectives that flow through the aisles and hallways, searching for clues and fondling spectators.*]

[*When she's done, the waitress skips behind the counter and begins to take Roarke's food away.*]

ROARKE: I didn't eat that.

WAITRESS: Nonetheless.

ROARKE: I'm not paying for that.

WAITRESS: You are paying for everything. You might as well order something you want. Preferably you will order something you desire.

ROARKE: *Want* and *desire* constitute the same line of flight. *Need*, on the other hand, is its own special becoming-animal. You meant to say *need*, I think.

WAITRESS [*rebooting*]: Would you like to hear our special today?

ROARKE: No.

WAITRESS: The special is a grilled cheese.

ROARKE: That's it?

WAITRESS: The special is a grilled cheese.

ROARKE: I heard you.

WAITRESS: The special . . . is a grilled cheese.

ROARKE: I said I heard you. Christ.

WAITRESS: The special . . .

ROARKE: . . . is a grilled cheese. Thank you. I said I heard you, goddamn it . . . Well, what else?

WAITRESS: What else.

ROARKE: Yes. What else? What else comes with the goddamn grilled cheese? Am I just supposed to eat the thing by itself? That's not a meal. That's a sandwich.

[*The waitress's jaw drops open like a coin dispenser.*]

ROARKE [*dejectedly*]: Hey. I'm talking to you. What else comes with the grilled cheese? Tomato soup? Pickles? Potato chips? Soda pop? And what's the grilled cheese made of? What kind of cheese? What kind of bread? What kind of butter do the cooks use to sauté it in the pan? Unsweetened or sweetened? I don't like unsweetened butter. What's the point? Incidentally most grilled cheeses aren't grilled cheeses. They're sautéed cheeses. Who grills a grilled cheese on a grill? It's unheard of.

WAITRESS [*closing her jaw*]: I don't know. The cooks don't tell me everything. [*Pauses.*] The usual bread, I suppose. [*Pauses.*] The cheese will either be yellow or white—that's a guarantee. [*Pauses.*] The other items you mentioned may be purchased à la carte. We don't have any sweet pickles.

ROARKE: Sweet pickles? Who the hell eats sweet pickles with a grilled cheese? Who eats sweet pickles with anything? They're disgusting. The fact that sweet pickles even exist is an atrocity.

WAITRESS: Clients often request sweet pickles. I hate to disappoint them.

ROARKE: Clients?

WAITRESS [*rebooting*]: Would you like to hear our special today?

ROARKE: What's wrong with you? You're acting funny. No— not funny. Your acting *affected*. Affectedness is a terrible character trait. Dystopian in its scope. I'd rather eat a jar of sweet pickles than sustain a moment's worth of affectedness.

WAITRESS [*rebooting*]: Let me clear these plates away for you.

Cold food is no food.

[*She puts the plates on a large platter and hurriedly takes them into the kitchen.*]

ROARKE [*to himself*]: I want a grilled cheese. But I NEED a mimosa.

WAITRESS [*backstage*]: Need? Don't you mean you WANT a mimosa, which is to say, DESIRE a mimosa, just as you WANT or DESIRE a grilled cheese? If you don't get a mimosa, nothing will happen. You will continue to exist. Hence need has nothing to do with it.

ROARKE [*sobbing*]: Bring me a goddamn mimosa! Bring me a goddamn grilled cheese! Don't bring me any goddamn side dishes! No sweet pickles! If I so much as smell a goddamn sweet pickle, I'm going to kill myself!

[*Silence.*]

INTERMEZZO

[*Roarke lays his head on the counter and closes his eyes. The theremin returns for a swan song, its eerie notes floating across the theater like drunken storks. The song sounds vaguely like "Over the Rainbow" from* The Wizard of Oz . . . *It is interrupted by an explosion of white noise that scrambles all of the superscreens. We see figures either having sex or bludgeoning one another behind the static. The theater lights flicker on and off, slowly at first, then rapidly, producing a stroboscopic effect. Strange creatures fly overhead. They could be pterodactyls, giant manta rays, or hang gliders. The occasional squawk evolves into a volley of gibbers and screeches. Soon there are monkeys and apes swinging back and forth across the theater on vines as armadillos scurry up the walls and salamanders and frogs rain from the ceiling in a bona fide jungle frenzy.*]

[*Somebody in a Trans Am roars onto the stage and fishtails across it, revving the engine and running over tables and diners. The windows of the car are tinted and we can only see the silhouette of the driver, which bears a striking resemblance to the profile of Roarke's therapist with his large skull, pointed beard, high forehead and wild hair.*]

[*As the Trans Am exits, stage left, a 3-D electroholographic display illuminates on the ceiling of the theater and reveals the cosmos. CAMERA DARTS through space at FTL speed, freezeframing near planets and moons, playing in the exhaust fumes of comets, diving into wormholes, bouncing across the surface of stars and supernovas like a skipping stone, etc. . . . XLS on a planet that looks like earth, but the land formations are different, resembling a flight of eroding butterflies pinned to a blue corkboard. SHUTTER-DISSOLVE to a CLOSER SHOT. After a few beats, the planet is struck by an asteroid that sets it on fire.*]

[*The overhead display collapses into a pulsing pinpoint of green light that moves across the ceiling like an EEG flatline and disappears into the topmost superscreen, which subsequently turns back on.*]

YOSHI

[*FADE IN to a TRACKING SHOT through the corridors and atriums of the mall. An offbeat idiom of champagne music accompanies the shot and is periodically interrupted by a crash of cymbals and electrostatic. Shoppers are aware of the camera. When it glides by, some of them ogle it in horror, as if witnessing an evisceration. The camera is innocuous at first and doesn't hit anybody, but then it clips a few shoppers, and soon it actively pursues and runs them over. Sirens go off and there is a period of all-purpose mayhem.*]

[*CAMERA DERAILS & SLINGSHOTS to the therapist's office. We skid into slowtime on the approach. Our POV drifts through a cluster of ersatz palm trees and closes on the office like a feather in the wind. On the left is a Yankee Candle store, on the right a Banana Republic. Both feature colorful articles of merchandise in their front windows whereas the therapist's office has tinted windows.*]

[*As we move closer, we see the therapist's signature and the name of his practice etched onto the door.*]

THE BETTER WELLNESS BUREAU
DR. G. STERNUM CURD, PH.D.
LICENSED PSYCHOTHERAPIST

[*We pass through the door with a shriek of electrostatic.*]

[*Darkness. CAMERA PICKS UP SPEED until a faint light becomes visible in the distance. We are in a wide hallway at the end of which is an oversized baroque fireplace with a phalanx of golden organ pipes rising from the mantelpiece. The fireplace hisses with flames that form a corona of light around the therapist, who sits in front of the fire. Arms resting comfortably in his lap, he occupies the middle of three conjoined home theater chairs. The other chairs are empty. Several misshapen clocks hang on the wall to the right and seem to be deliquescing into the plaster. Shadows play against the lefthand wall; on several occasions, we perceive the silhouette of a Slender Man, treebranch arms reaching across the office.*]

[*Slowly we drift forward to an EXTREME CLOSE UP on the therapist's solarized face. HOLD on the face.*]

[*The skin bears no imperfections—no pockmarks, discolorations, scars, bumps or cysts. There is a kind of sheen or glaze to the skin, almost like a wax figure or mannequin, but it doesn't look unnatural.*

A slightly off-center vein runs from his feral brow to the beachfront of a full but receded hairline. His beard is trim and thick, like turf. Firelight dances against the lenses of his pince-nez as he gazes down at the audience. He is at once a god and a clown.]

[*The therapist's face is stoic, immobile. He does not blink. Sometimes he experiences a small tic or convulsion at the eye and mouth corners. On occasion his entire head judders and vibrates like a possessed fist. Whenever this happens, a theremin detonates offstage.*]

[*During the overhead interludes, diners that have been run over by the Trans Am moan quietly and reach out for help. Most of them are dead. Diners that the Trans Am didn't run over sit at their tables and booths like short-circuited robots.*]

[*The stagelights flutter and there is a gunshot.*]

[*A row of shirtless bodies fall from the overhead copper pipes on nooses. They have been fitted in black hoods and bound at the wrists and ankles. None of their necks break. Dangling, they wriggle and squirm until they suffocate and go limp.*]

[*Another gunshot validates the executions and signals the extras onstage. Dead or alive, the diners get up, fall into sequence and exit, stage right, in an orderly line. There is no disturbance in the GOOD-SCREEN, but we hear aqueous swallowing noises.*]

[*The therapist's head spasms and another theremin suffers the consequences. Roarke lifts his head from the counter, opens his eyes and glances vacantly around the ruins of the diner.*]

ROARKE [*yawning, rubbing his temples*]: Mimosa . . . Mimosa . . . Mimosa. [*He sighs . . . then screams until his larynx gives out.*]

[*The waitress exits the kitchen carrying a platter that contains a grilled cheese, tomato soup and pickles. She wears lingerie and walks with a limp. She looks older. Her skin is wrinkled. Her hair has fallen apart and is mostly gray now.*]

ROARKE: What the hell happened to you? You look like a goddamn train wreck. [*He double-takes her.*] I like your uniform. It suits you.

WAITRESS [*putting the food on the counter*]: One grilled cheese, one bowl of tomato soup, one side order of pickles. Dill.

ROARKE: I didn't order all of this! Where's the mimosa?

WAITRESS: The diner doesn't serve mimosas. Would you like a Bloody Mary?

ROARKE [*taken aback*]: Bloody Mary? That doesn't make any sense. [*Tentatively he tastes a pickle, then spits it out.*] Christ! That's a goddamn sweet pickle! [*Tentatively he tastes the soup, then spits it out.*] Disgusting! That tastes like goddamn hell! [*He inspects the grilled cheese, opening and closing it.*] This looks all right. I wouldn't expect the diner to offer marbled pumpernickel bread, let alone what smells like Gouda cheese. Is that Gouda cheese? It might be Fontina. I wonder what kind of butter the cook used to brown the out-facing sides of the bread. Maybe he used oil, but that's preposterous. One uses butter to brown the exterior of a grilled cheese. That isn't to say cooking oil wouldn't work. It *would* work—and it would work very, very well. But there's something to be said for tradition. I assume butter came before cooking oil. Thus prehistoric cooks used butter to make grilled cheeses, and when cooking oil came along, they said why fix what ain't broke? You know what I mean.

WAITRESS: You're stalling.

ROARKE: I know. In spite of everything, I'm worried that I'll have the same experience with the grilled cheese that I had with the tomato soup and the pickles. But wait: I'll give the soup a second chance. [*Furiously he sprinkles shakers of pepper and salt on the soup and takes another sip. Moaning, he spews it over his shoulder.*] I've used salt and pepper to save countless meals. Nothing will save that soup. Well. I can't bring myself to try the grilled cheese. One more disappointment will be my endgame. I don't want to die disappointed.

WAITRESS: Would you like me to throw a fried egg on that grilled cheese?

ROARKE [*baffled*]: Fried egg? I don't understand.

WAITRESS: I'll have the cook throw a fried egg on that grilled cheese for you. You'll like it.

ROARKE: Fried egg? Are you goddamn crazy? Who puts a fried egg on a grilled cheese? It's unheard of.

WAITRESS: You'll like it. A fried egg can significantly enhance the flavor and consequent enjoyment of a grilled cheese. Trust me on this one.

ROARKE: Consequent enjoyment? What language is that?

WAITRESS: I'll tell the cook to put it right on top. I'll tell him to drape it over the roof of the grilled cheese like a wet handkerchief. No—like an elastic puddle. No—like a flattened eyeball. *Un globe oculaire aplatie.*

ROARKE: Can I PLEASE have a mimosa for the love of God? I know they're back there. [*He cups a hand to his mouth and shouts at the kitchen.*] I know you've got mimosas back there!

WAITRESS: Have you ever eaten a cheese omelet with a side of toast? It's the same thing.

ROARKE: No it's not. It's an entirely different thing. The arrangement of things is *everything*. An omelet and toast has nothing to do with a grilled cheese and a fried egg. You're talking about two different entities altogether. It doesn't matter if the core ingredients are the same. Joseph Stalin had the same core ingredients as me. DNA and bones and nerve bundles and so forth. Stalin, however, became a politician, warlord and mass murderer, whereas I became Me.

WAITRESS: Let me get a fried egg for you. You'll feel better. I'll be right back.

[*She clears the plates and limps to the kitchen. During her absence, the holographic ghost of Big Rita rumbles back and forth across the stage like a berserk linebacker with nobody to tackle. The ghost is twice the size of the original Big Rita and screams twice as loud, prompting the therapist on the ÜBERSCREEN to scream in retaliation. Roarke covers his ears and barks at Big Rita and the therapist but we can't hear him.*]

[*The therapist screams until he runs out of air, then takes a deep, stertorous breath and screams again, the vein on his forehead swelling and wriggling like a stepped-on snake. This goes on until he loses consciousness and slides from the chair and out of view, at which point the ghost of Big Rita bursts into glittering cyphers that rise to the ceiling. The therapist never returns. On the ÜBERSCREEN, the lazy flames of the fire crackle softly behind the empty chair.*]

[*There is a hydraulic crunch and all of the power in the theater goes out. The roar of intricate machines follows a litany of explosions.*]

[*When the power comes back on, both the ÜBERSCREEN and the PORTSCREEN display colorful test patterns that emit dull, deadened whistles. The GOODSCREEN remains a swamp of molten blobs. The stage is empty, barren; the entire diner is gone—all of the appliances, decorations, furniture, the counter, etc.—even the rhomboidal walls and ceiling that defined it have been removed. The floor of the stage angles into a backdrop of cartoon BLUENESS.*]

[*Naked, Roarke stands center stage, dumbly, facing the GOOD-SCREEN. After awhile the waitress staggers out of the BLUENESS. She is naked, too, and very elderly now, a bag of wrinkles shrink-wrapped to a broken cross. She can barely walk. Pretending to carry a plate in her hands, she ambles downstage and turns to Roarke.*]

WAITRESS: One grilled cheese capped with a fried egg. Paper covers rock, as they say.

ROARKE [*snipping his fingers together*]: I didn't order that.

WAITRESS: Try it. You'll thank yourself.

ROARKE: I might as well give it a try. [*He pretends to take the grilled cheese from the plate and bite into it. He chews with relish.*] You're right. The grilled cheese is delicious and the fried egg really enhances the flavor and my consequent enjoyment of it. Thank you.

WAITRESS: You're welcome.

ROARKE: I'm glad I have this mimosa to wash it down. I've been looking forward to it. I drank too much last night. I mixed the liquor and the wine and I chainsmoked eight cigars. That's not a good combination. A mimosa will certainly hit the spot.

WAITRESS: Without question, hitting the spot is the ultimate truth. There's nothing more important.

ROARKE: I agree. [*Pretending to hold a large goblet, he tilts back his head and gulps loudly.*] That might be the best mimosa I ever tasted in my life.

WAITRESS: The cook uses pomegranate juice instead of orange juice. He also includes a dash of lukewarm sake in addition to the champagne.

ROARKE: Genius. That explains it. [*He drinks from the invisible goblet again, tosses it aside and wipes his lips with the back of a hand.*] Christ. I feel like a new goddamn man.

WAITRESS: That makes me happy. I've always wanted the best for you. [*She hands him an invisible slip of paper.*] Here's your bill.

ROARKE: Thank you. [*He reads the bill.*] Eight hundred and seventy-five dollars and twenty-four cents. That sounds reasonable. Everything appears to be in order. I'll pay you in cash. Will a thousand dollar bill cover it?

WAITRESS: That's not quite a 20% tip.

ROARKE: You're right. Here, take two thousand dollars. The service was really good.

WAITRESS: Thank you. We pride ourselves on good service at the diner.

[*The lights flicker and produce another stroboscopic effect.*]

ROARKE: It's time.

WAITRESS: Yes.

ROARKE: Take your top off.

WAITRESS: Ok. [*She pretends to take her top off*]. There.

ROARKE: Take your skirt off.

WAITRESS: Ok. [*She pretends to take her skirt off.*] There.

ROARKE: Take your bra and your underwear off.

WAITRESS: What about you?

ROARKE: You first.

WAITRESS: Ok. [*She pretends to take her underwear and bra off.*] The clasp is stuck. Can you help me?

ROARKE: Of course. [*She turns around and he unclasps her bra*]. There.

WAITRESS: Thank you. Now you.

ROARKE: Ok. [*He pretends to take his clothes off.*] I wonder what our children will be like. And I wonder what they'll look like. I try to envision them on my mind's screen but there are no contours, no features, no shadows or outcroppings on their faces.

WAITRESS: They will be beautiful. You are a beautiful man.

ROARKE: Thank you. We'll call our children Roarke, Jr. All of them. Girls and boys. We'll live on a hill in Scandinavia and we'll live there forever. You can still wait tables. We'll find a nice pub or a discotheque for you in the town at the bottom of the hill.

WAITRESS: That sounds like utopia.

ROARKE: It doesn't matter to me that you work in the service industry. You know that, right?

WAITRESS: Yes. I know.

ROARKE: We should probably lie down now. Don't forget to spread your legs and close your eyes.

WAITRESS: I won't.

ROARKE: Just to be clear: I don't love you.

WAITRESS: I know. I don't love you either.

ROARKE: I don't love anybody. Not even Myself.

WAITRESS: I know. Love is impossible. There's nothing meaningful or logical to say about it.

ROARKE: Yes.

WAITRESS: To say you love somebody is an act of Unbeing. The moment the word "love" escapes one's lips is the moment one devolves into imbecility.

ROARKE: Lie down.

WAITRESS: Love is an imaginary phenomenon.

ROARKE: Lie down.

WAITRESS: Love is an illusory fantasy, a specular mirage, an autoerotic deception.

ROARKE: Lie down.

WAITRESS: Love belongs to the matrix of the Ego.

ROARKE: Please lie down.

WAITRESS: The metaphor of love is that thing we think we point at inside of somebody else, but in fact it is only that which we point at inside ourselves. And our insides are defined by *lack*.

ROARKE: Please lie down.

WAITRESS: Desire is the thing.

ROARKE: Please?

WAITRESS: Desire for the desire for desire.

ROARKE: I want to make love to you.

[*The waitress screams.*]

ROARKE [*groaning in consternation*]: I love you.

[*Brief tableau.*]

WAITRESS: I love you too. Lie down.

[*As they get on the floor, the stage lights flicker out in synch with the* ÜBERSCREEN *and* PORTSCREEN. *The* GOODSCREEN *remains illuminated for several beats, then irises off.*]

CURTAIN

THE DARK HYPOTENUSE

CHARACTERS

Starke
Screaming Man
Old Man
Baby
Fleeting-Improvised Man
Therapist
Mrs. Starke
Flang
King Bun a.k.a. Judge Bun a.k.a. Bun
Townspeople
Circusfolk
Elephant
Elephant Handler
Bailiff
Prosecuting Attorney
Defense Attorney
Court Officers
Court Secretary
Jury
Mayor
Paramedics
Lawyers
Veterinarian
Pigs
Apes
Fishes
Mannequins
Mercy-Begger/Giver
Medical Students
Homunculus
Nathanial Hörnblowér
Deconstructionists
Flang's Girlfriend
Dentist
Dental Assistant
Henchman #1
Henchman #2
Henchman #3
Screaming Pope

SCHIZE

This one-act schematism involves a middle-aged man with a hangover who accidentally steps into what may or may not be the Lacanian Real. The stage is a thick black rhombus that hovers in the middle of the theater. The floor is a maze of trap doors through which actors may enter or exit. Some of the trap doors swing open whereas others slide or fall open. Giant mechanical arms extend from underneath of the stage. At the end of each arm is a gondola that sits up to ten spectators. Throughout the performance, the arms are in constant motion and move the audience all over the theater so that each gondola achieves a fluid multiperspectivalism as it glides east to west, north to south, accomplishing close-ups and bird's-eye views and everything in between.

The Lacanian Real is the impossible, impenetrable realm around which the world turns like a berserk Möbius strip. Together with the orders of the Imaginary and the Symbolic, the Real completes a triangulation of intra-psychic phenomena that take their cue from Freud's theories of infantile sexuality, the Oedipal phase, and disentombing unconscious flows of desire via the technology of language. The Imaginary constitutes the realm of the ego and the specular image, functioning as a platform for their dual relationship, which perpetually unfolds across the Mind's Screen, whereas the Symbolic involves the associative formation of signifiers and signifieds (i.e., the realm of language). Not to be confused with "the real" a.k.a. "reality," the Real (with a capital R) emerges as that which cannot be represented, that which is pre-Imaginary, pre-Symbolic, or, as it were, that which contradicts the Imaginary and transcends the Symbolic while remaining intimately bound to these orders. The play is situated on the unfathomable surface of this very trauma center.

It should be noted that certain demographics collectively refer to the Lacanian Real as the Dark Hypotenuse.

At the end of each scene, the theater darkens completely and the gondolas accelerate to a dizzying speed, nauseating their occupants. When a new act begins, the lights come on and the gondolas return to their normal speed and behavior.

[PRODUCTION NOTE: In the event that the technology is unavailable and/or unaffordable, the play may be set in an arena theater wherein a deep, dark trench surrounds the stage. Preferably each row of seats will turn at erratic intervals on the axis of the stage like the planets of the Copernican solar system. Conversely the stage may turn while the seats remain fixed. Ideally everything will turn—stage and seats, actors and audience, always in the opposite direction.]

SCENE 1
Starke, Screaming Man
The Lacanian Real.

[Dressed in a brown, tight-fitting, three-piece suit, Starke stands center stage covertly sniffing his armpits, one after the other. He can't seem to decide if they smell badly or not. A trap door swings open and a screaming man tries to crawl out of it. He gets stuck. He screams louder and calls out to Starke for help.]

STARKE: *Siparium.*

SCREAMING MAN: Help me out of this goddamn hole! Holy hell! I can't get out! Good lord!

STARKE [*bending over*]: Take my hand. [*He doesn't offer the screaming man his hand.*]

SCREAMING MAN: Help! Help! Help! Help! Help! Help! Help! Help! Help! Help!

[*Starke reaches out and slams the trap door shut on the screaming man's head. The scream dopplers into the Abyss.*]

STARKE [*standing*]: That is not what I had planned to do.

SCENE 2
Old Man, Baby
Nowhere.

[*An elderly man with a white pompadour hairdo drags a baby by the tail of a onesie with one hand. The baby squirms and cries softly as the man ambles forward, punching the stage with the butt of a cane that he maneuvers with his other hand. He goes back and forth for some time, as if lost but not really concerned about it, then pauses in a stage corner and tries to speak. He can't. He clears his throat and tries to speak again. Fails. The baby cries louder as he repeatedly tries and fails to say something; the best he can do is emit powerful croaks. Finally he lets go of the onesie and throws his body into the effort of articulation, which offsets him. Strained, he clutches his chest, doubles over and falls off the stage. The baby shrieks louder and louder as the old man, moaning like a stabbed goat, dopplers into the Abyss.*]

SCENE 3
Starke
Somewhere.

STARKE [*peering over the edge of the stage*]: Good riddance you son of a bitch! [*He loses balance and waves his arms helplessly. He nearly falls over, then catches himself, pivots and marches towards the center stage . . .*]

SCENE 4
Starke
Somewhere else.

[*Starke paces from one side of the stage to the other, gesticulating and crying out like a Tourette's patient.*]

STARKE [*pausing*]: When you are in doubt—wait for the future to unbury you.

[*A trap door opens beneath him. Swallows him.*]

SCENE 5
Starke, Fleeting-Improvised Man
A clearing.

[*Starke crawls out of one trap door and into another, scurrying across the stage on all fours like a frenzied insect. This goes on for awhile. Finally, standing, he pats down his vest and sleeves and straightens his tie.*]

STARKE [*glancing about the theater*]: Bartender? Bartender!

[*A large suitcase falls from the ceiling and nearly lands on Starke. He cries out and jumps aside. He tries to hide . . . but there's nothing to hide behind or under. Pacing backwards, he grips his mouth with both hands and stifles a scream. His panic escalates when the suitcase begins to move and hop around like a jumping bean. Someone or something is inside of it trying to punch or kick or claw its way out. We hear a lot of growling. Then a voice.*]

FLEETING-IMPROVISED MAN: Help me out of this goddamn box! Holy hell! I can't get out! Good lord!

[*Starke finds the courage to approach the suitcase. As the entity inside becomes more agitated, he fumbles with the zipper, but it won't open. He fumbles with a latch. It won't open either.*

FLEETING-IMPROVISED MAN: What the hell are you doing! Get me out of here!

STARKE: I'm trying! It's locked! It's stuck! It won't open! I don't know what to do!

FLEETING-IMPROVISED MAN: Help! Help! Help! Help! Help! Help! Help! Help! Help!

[*The suitcase leaps up, hits Starke in the chin and knocks him onto his back. Dazed, he gets to his feet, bellows angrily, and kicks the suitcase as hard as he can. It tumbles halfway across the stage, springs open like a mousetrap and unleashes a howling geyser of dirty laundry. Starke tries to avoid the clothes, but they fall everywhere, and they seem to attack him, wrapping around his limbs and especially his face, as if to suffocate him. He trips and falls several times while he tears himself free. Eventually the clothes stop antagonizing him and lay still.*]

[*As Starke catches his breath, a man slowly emerges from a pile of clothes. He is a mirror image of Starke, only naked and hairless, and his skin is glossy. He flickers on and off.*]

STARKE [*terrified*]: Are . . . are you who I am?

FLEETING-IMPROVISED MAN: No. I am only who you are not.

THERAPIST [*somewhere offstage*]: The Dark Hypotenuse knows no equal. There can only be one Un-Word, one Undifferentiation, one Unfathomable Truth. Everything else is the flotsam and jetsam of Ego.

[*Starke attacks the fleeting-improvised man, but when he puts his hands on him, the fleeting-improvised man deliquesces. Starke screams until he runs out of air, then screams again . . .*]

SCENE 6
Starke, Mrs. Starke, Flang, King Bun
Grandfather's attic.

STARKE: I hate it up here in grandpa's attic. That old bastard is sleeping in the dirt and here we are sucking on his dust. King Bun! Bring me the cleaning spray!

MRS. STARKE [*cradling a half-naked man in a rocking chair*]: King Bun is sleeping. Listen to him purr, Starke.

STARKE: That sounds more like silence than noise, Mrs. Starke. This place is filthy. Flang! The featherduster!

[*Flang is a chimpanzee. He wears the same three-piece suit as Starke and resembles a kind of diminutive, devolved, hirsute version of him.*

At the ready, he leaps onto a dresser, retrieves a featherduster from a drawer, leaps off and bounds over to Starke.]

STARKE: Thank you, sir. At least two of us are worth the price of marbles and salt. [*Takes the featherduster and begins cleaning the furniture.*]

[*King Bun cries out in his sleep.*]

MRS. STARKE [*caressing him*]: Shh. It's all right, King Bun. It's just the nightmare of reality.

FLANG [*screeching*]: Put a muzzle on that king or I will eat him! That's a promise!

STARKE: Flang! Mind your tongue. No matter how you slice it, you're still a monkey. [*Frustrated.*] This featherduster isn't working. The dust is permanent. It's not coming off!

[*King Bun spasms and almost knocks Mrs. Starke out of the rocker.*]

MRS. STARKE: Quiet, Starke! You're waking up King Bun!

STARKE: This is my grandfather's attic! I'll do as I please, when I please, if only to spite the Deceased and the Earth.

FLANG: Down with King Bun!

STARKE: Flang! What did I just tell you!

MRS. STARKE: King Bun's arm is going to fall off again!

STARKE: No it's not!

MRS. STARKE: It's going to fall off! You're making it happen!

STARKE: I'm not making anything happen! That arm has a mind of it's own!

MRS. STARKE: Oh no!

[*As he continues to jitter in Mrs. Starke's lap, King Bun's arm falls off, as if it had been poorly screwed on. The loss jars him awake. He shrieks and lashes out and he and Mrs. Starke fall backwards out of the rocker.*]

STARKE: Holy Freud! Somebody man the helm!

[*Hooting, Flang scurries across the stage, retrieves the arm and hurls it at a gondola of spectators that passes overhead. The act of aggression completely maddens King Bun, who, still shrieking, convulses and flops across the stage while Mrs. Starke flails on her back like an overturned tortoise.*]

STARKE: Good show, Flang! Your aim is getting better every day. Now I think I might take a nap. All this filth and excitement—it hangs heavy on a man's consciousness. [*Collapses.*]

SCENE 7A
Starke, Townspeople, Circusfolk, Elephant, Elephant Handler
A street in Dreamfield, Indiana.

[*Led by a drunken four-piece band, a traveling circus parades in a circle around the stage as bystanders clap and cheer. Starke is among them, although he watches the procession idly, with no expression. Acrobats somersault and fly in and out of trap doors.*]

[*An elephant playing a musical horn with its trunk towers above the many other attractions. Unhappy with the performance, a handler screams at the elephant, ordering it to play louder, better. The elephant tries harder, but the handler is incorrigible and begins to jab it with a pitchfork in the legs and belly. The elephant roars. Its trunk contorts and lashes out and drops the horn. The handler snaps. Determined to kill the elephant, he lunges at its chest to stab it in the heart. The elephant's skin is too thick for the pitchfork to penetrate it, but the handler draws blood, and at the sight of it, the elephant rears back on its hind legs, trunk flailing and swatting the handler aside. Then it drops onto its forelegs and stomps on the handler's head. Blood and brains squirt from the foot. Terrified spectators scream and flee the scene, throwing themselves offstage and dopplering into the Abyss en masse. A number of circusfolk follow suit while some of them try in vain to restore order.*]

[*Starke approaches the elephant and pets and strokes its trunk. The elephant kneels. He caresses its ears and head.*]

STARKE [*weeping*]: I'm sorry, my friend. I have to let you go.

SCENE 7B
Starke, Bailiff, Court Secretary, Court Officers, Defense Attorney, Prosecuting Attorney, Judge Bun, Elephant, Jury
A courtroom in Dreamfield, Indiana.

BAILIFF: Order in the court! Judge Bun presiding.

STARKE [*distraught*]: That's not a judge! That's King Bun! That's my boy!

[*Judge Bun falls out of his chair.*]

BAILIFF: Silence! One more outburst like that, sir, and I will send you home to your wife!

STARKE: You can't send me home to my wife! You're a goddamn bailiff! Mind the King, please. Help my son.

[*The bailiff steps onto the dais and lifts Judge Bun into his chair. Flaccid, he falls out again. The bailiff puts him back, removes the belt from his trousers, wraps it around Judge Bun's chest and secures the buckle behind the chair. Judge Bun's head tips to one side. He drools onto his shoulder and stares blankly into space.*]

BAILIFF: Order in the court.

STARKE: Nobody's out of order except you and the secretary. She's sleeping, the old bat.

BAILIFF [*whispering*]: Don't wake her. She's irritable when she's groggy and there's no coffee.

[*The elephant moans. The defense attorney pets its trunk and tries to soothe it as six court officers tighten their grips on the ropes that bind it.*]

PROSECUTING ATTORNEY: Your honor, I motion to have this beast removed from the courtroom. We've already seen what it's capable of! [*He points at the table where the smashed brains of the handler have been gathered into a glass jar.*]

[*Traumatized, the elephant rears onto its hind legs with the intention of stomping on the jar and the prosecuting attorney. The court officers shock it with prods until it returns to all fours with a great thud. It blows its trunk and falls silent.*]

STARKE [*to the court officers*]: Stop doing that, you dirty sons of bitches! If you antagonized me I'd stomp on you too. Who wouldn't?

BAILIFF: That's enough out of you! Bailiff, secure the witness.

[*The Bailiff grabs Starke and they wrestle around and punch each other in the faces.*]

STARKE: You can't tell yourself what to do you! You can't tell yourself what to do!

BAILIFF: How dare you insult the viability of this trial! Bailiff, suplex the witness.

STARKE [*upside-down in the air*]: I'm not a witness! I'm a spectator! Don't suplex me!

[*The bailiff accomplishes a suplex and Starke slams into the floor.*]

BAILIFF [*standing*]: Are you saying that you didn't see what happened? Is that what you're saying?

[*Starke groans and vomits.*]

BAILIFF: Right. Mr. Prosecutor?

PROSECUTING ATTORNEY: Thank you, sir. And thank you, Judge Bun. I'd like to take this chance to thank the jury for their time. I promise that nobody will be disappointed in the proceedings that are on the cusp of unfolding like the smooth stain-free sheets of a king-sized bed at a five-star hotel. Not since I single-handedly impeached Dr. Cornelius from the Office of the Presidency have I felt so adamant about a case.

[*He points at the elephant.*] This gigantic and deranged mammal stomped on a man's head and turned his think-machine into oatmeal! Everybody saw it happen. There's no question as to the guilt of said gigantic and deranged mammal. I dare say—

[*King Bun screams and slams down a gavel, awakening the secretary. She screams. The elephant swoons.*]

DEFENSE ATTORNEY: My client is having a nervous breakdown! The breakdown is a direct effect of the proceedings taking place at this moment. Stop screaming, for God's sake! [*King Bun and the secretary fall silent.*] Thank you. I declare a mistrial at once. My client is clearly under duress and being taken advantage of by mankind. Don't make me sue this court. I won't hesitate! I will put mankind on the stand and reduce him to bitter tears. I will—

[*King Bun slams down the gavel. The secretary punches her typewriter and bleats.*]

COURT SECRETARY: We all know where this is going! I sentence that miserable elephant to Hell! Hell by hanging. It is so. [*She bleats again.*]

[*King Bun slams down the gavel and escapes the security of the bailiff's belt. Coincidentally the bailiff's pants fall down. The jury laughs. The prosecuting attorney shoots the defense attorney. The court officers prod the elephant, but it is numb at this point, shell-shocked by the declaration of its fate.*]

SCENE 7C
Starke, Elephant, Mayor, Paramedics, Lawyers, Veterinarian,
Townspeople
An abandoned drive-in theater in Dreamfield, Indiana.

[*Starke's cinematic unconscious flits across a movie screen that looms over the western edge of the stage. The torrent of imagery is dominated by still shots and stock footage of war, pornography and Red Carpet bacchanalia. There are also clips from home movies, commercials, sitcoms, satellite recordings of deep space, and Hitchcock films. No soundtrack accompanies the cerebral carnival. It is aggressive and uninterrupted and silent.*]

[*A railcar-mounted industrial crane occupies the eastern wing of the stage. Starke crouches behind the stick-shift controls. Beneath the crane is a shivering elephant. A thick chain extends from the upper boom to a noose wrapped around the elephant's neck.*]

[*Between the screen and the crane, bloodthirsty townspeople have worked themselves into a minor frenzy. The children are far more irate and belligerent than the adults, swearing at the elephant and throwing toys and rocks and bibles at it.*]

STARKE: This is not what I had planned to do! This is not what I had planned to do!

TOWNSPEOPLE [*chanting*]: Kill the mastodon! Kill the mastodon! Kill the mastodon!

STARKE: That's not a mastodon, you goddamn heathens! Do you see any shag on that mammal? Burn in hell! [*To the elephant, leaning out of the crane.*] This is not what I had planned to do. Ignore these troglodytes.

[*Starke manipulates the controls and slowly lifts the elephant into the air by the neck. It screams a human scream and blows its trunk as it rises off of its forelegs. Its extremities gesticulate like unmanned firehoses when the crane lifts it completely off the stage and it begins to suffocate. The townspeople cheer. Starke moans but doesn't stop the crane; the elephant ascends into the heavens . . . Then the chain snaps and it plunges to the stage, crushing and killing at least twenty townspeople.*]

MAYOR [*raising a mug of beer*]: Cheers, mate.

[*Paramedics flow out of trap doors and flood the stage as the townspeople shriek in terror and form a violent mosh pit. The elephant's trunk slams down like a sledgehammer, claiming additional victims, then goes limp.*]

[*Four paramedics carry a veterinarian to the elephant on a throne. They dump him onto the elephant's head and the veterinarian climbs around its body, testing its clockwork with a stethoscope.*]

VETERINARIAN: She has a broken hip, but she's breathing normally. The old girl is still fit to hang.

[*The townspeople cheer. Starke swears in protest as he revs the engine of the crane. Frantic construction workers replace the chain and refasten the noose around the elephant's neck. Starke throws the contents of a toolbox at them. Usually he misses the mark, but on several occasions he pegs a worker with a wrench or screwdriver and the worker falls off the crane. When the job is done, the workers turn on Starke, threatening to kill him, but the mayor scares them off with a flame-thrower.*]

MAYOR [*securing the flame-thrower*]: Cheers, mates. If you please, then, Mr. Starke.

STARKE: Mr. Starke? There's no mister, you bag of shit. It's just plain Starke.

[*The townspeople boo.*]

[*The paramedics try to take Starke away on a stretcher, but he fights them off with a hammer. Finally he returns to the controls and begrudgingly lifts the elephant into the air again.*]

ELEPHANT [*in the echoic voice of a rector*]: I can feel it.

[*The elephant's tongue unrolls from its mouth like a carpet when it dies. The townspeople cheer . . . and all the trap doors spring open, flinging them offstage. Their cheers thread into shrieks as they doppler into the Abyss. The paramedics dive offstage to save them. The mayor waves to the potential voters in the gondolas that glide around him like electrons, then drops into a trap door.*]

[*Starke steps out of the crane. He's carrying a handgun. He walks to the center of the stage and looks up at the elephant. He aims the gun at it with a trembling arm. He whimpers. Screaming, he shoots the elephant in the head. It swings back and forth on the creaking chain.*]

SCENE 8
Starke, Mrs. Starke, Flang, King Bun
Grandfather's basement.

[*Mrs. Starke folds a pile of laundry on a table next to a loud washer and dryer as Flang and Starke look on. They almost have to shout to hear one another.*]

STARKE: It feels better to be down here in grandpa's basement. I can practically hear him breathing in the dirt. [*Listens.*] That dryer is a menace. What the hell's in that contraption? A lot of rocks and bones, if you ask me.

[*Flang unbuckles and pulls down his suit pants in an act of defiance.*]

STARKE: Flang! This isn't the House of Parliament. It's grandpa's basement! [*Rubbing his temples.*] By god, this hangover's going to be the death of me. And yet I've forgotten that I even have a hangover. I always have a hangover—thus it has become a normative condition.

MRS. STARK: Thus? Thus? Thus! [*Pauses.*] What?

STARKE: Stop that. What did your mother used to say was the best cure for normativity?

MRS. STARKE: Kindness?

STARKE: No, it wasn't kindness. If anything it was enmity. But it wasn't that either. I remember now. A banana, an onanism, and a two-hour nap—in that order, if memory serves. Something about the combination of potassium, masturbation and unconsciousness, your mother insisted, would wipe out a hangover, any hangover, no matter how powerful or resolute, with tsunamic efficiency. If only they could bottle it up.

FLANG [*pulling up his pants*]: They can. It's called Oxycodone. Start by washing down 40 milligrams with a glass a table wine and see where that puts you.

MRS. STARKE: Where is King Bun? I haven't seen him all day.

STARKE: Where am I supposed to get Oxycodone, Flang? You know I hate doctors.

FLANG: I can prescribe you a two-week supply of 10 milligram tablets, but I don't want you taking more than two per day. Is that clear?

MRS. STARKE: King Bun! King Bun! Hello! [*Listens.*] He's not answering.

STARKE: I don't want your drugs, Flang. Dog hair will suffice. Waitress!

MRS. STARKE: I'm starting to get worried about King Bun.

FLANG [*pretending to be a waitress*]: Coffee and water, then? [*To Mrs. Starke.*] King Bun is in the dryer, by the way. Again.

MRS. STARKE: What? Oh no!

STARKE [*to the audience*]: She keeps putting him in there and then she expects everything to be all right. I don't know what comes over her.

FLANG: Dry, King Bun! Dry! Dry!

[*Mrs. Starke trips and falls as she lunges for the dryer. She gets up, falls down, gets up and opens the dryer. King Bun tumbles out and loses an arm.*]

FLANG: There goes another arm. Huzzah!

[*Screaming, King Bun somersaults across the stage, falls off and dopplers into the Abyss.*]

MRS. STARKE: Oh my god! My son is dead!

STARKE: Not yet. I can still hear him falling. [*King Bun's scream dwindles to silence.*] Ok I think he's dead now. Anyway I can't hear him screaming anymore.

FLANG: At least he isn't wet anymore.

STARKE: Atta boy, Flang. Focus on the positive. Keep your eye on the sun.

MRS. STARKE [*running across the stage*]: I'll save you, King Bun! Mama's coming! [*Screaming, she dives off the edge and dopplers into the Abyss.*]

STARKE: Well I guess it's just you and me now, Flang. Are we grilling tonight or should I order takeout? I've got two ribeyes in the refrigerator with our names on them.

FLANG: I'm a vegetarian.

STARKE: That's preposterous. You ate veal for breakfast.

FLANG: I just became one.

STARKE: When?

FLANG: The moment I said I was.

STARKE: What's that supposed to mean?

FLANG: Meaning is subjective. It doesn't matter. Nothing does.

[*Screaming, Flang attacks Starke, leaping onto his shoulders and knocking him over. Starke screams, too, as Flang pounds his head into the stage.*]

[*Flang stops beating Starke and climbs off of him. They stand and calmly brush off their suits and straighten their ties.*]

FLANG: I'm worried about mother and King Bun. What if they don't come back this time?

STARKE: They'll come back. They always come back. You can kill your friends, but you can't kill your family.

[*A trap door falls open beneath Starke and claims him. Flang remains onstage. He stands there absently, glancing around the theater, then sits and cleans his feet and hands with his tongue.*]

SCENE 9
Pigs, Apes, Fishes
The great hall of the palace.

[*An assembly of pigs and apes wander listlessly among a dispersion of fishes that flop up and down in their death throes. Occasionally an ape makes an attempt to mount and ride a pig, and sometimes a pig tramples an ape, but for the most part they ignore each other. They are as lost as they are dazed and apathetic.*]

SCENE 10
Mannequins, Fishes
The great hall of the palace.

[*Repeat the last scene, only instead of pigs and apes, the stage is full of mannequins situated in poses that indicate enthusiasm, intellect, and team spirit. They wear a variety of clothes from different time periods. Several of the mannequins' are headless and their neckholes emit ominous vapors.*]

SCENE 11
Starke, Mrs. Starke, Flang, King Bun
Grandmother's kitchen.

STARKE: Stop saying that, Flang. Mrs. Starke does not have a cloaca. You're just being rude for the sake of being rude now. You're just like your grandpa, god rest his shriveled soul. Rude without purpose.

[*An egg drops from Mrs. Starke's skirt and rolls across the stage. King Bun sits nearby, staring into space. He claps dumbly.*]

MRS. STARKE: Oh my goodness!

[*Several more eggs drop and roll from the skirt.*]

FLANG: Aha!

[*Knuckle-scuttling after the eggs, Flang tries to stomp on and pound them. Somehow the eggs evade him. Starke tackles Flang and boxes his ears.*]

STARKE: Nobody destroys my babies but me! I'll send you back to the jungle, Flang. Count on it!

MRS. STARKE [*clutching her skirt*]: Don't talk to him like that, Starke! That's not how we agreed to raise our churlin! The mere indication, let alone the threat, of jungle-banishment is an act of abuse and molestation.

STARKE: Churlin shmurlin. Calm down, Mrs. Starke. That goes for everybody. Everybody stop screaming and carrying on! This is grandma's kitchen. You know how she hated strife, god rest her blessed soul.

[*Flang snickers. Starke boxes his ears again, gets up and kicks him in the groin.*]

STARKE: I won't send you to the jungle, Flang! I'll cook you and I'll eat you! I'll roast you like a chicken in the stove!

MRS. STARKE: Starke! Stop it!

STARKE: Apologies, wife. Anyway we better collect these eggs before they roll into the Abyss. King Bun? Please do the honors.

[*King Bun tries to obey but his motor skills are underdeveloped and he can't even crawl. The best he can do is fall over and reach out.*]

STARKE: Well done, King Bun. It's true what they say. There's more than one way to fry an egg.

[*As the eggs continue to roll, something inside each of them emits an insect scream. One at a time, they fall off the stage and doppler into the Abyss. Mrs. Starke screams and another egg falls out of her skirt. It splats between her feet. She screams harder, taking deep inhalations between each outbreath.*]

SCENE 12
Mercy-Beggers, Mercy-Givers
The Infinite Plateau.

[*Two men carrying M4 Carbine assault rifles emerge from opposing trap doors. They look like Starke. Pointing the guns, they begin to shout at and chase one another across the stage. One man gets cornered. He drops to his knees, hugs the gun to his chest and begs for mercy. Reluctantly, the other man acquiesces, and at that moment the mercy-begger shoots him. It's not a mortal wound and the chase resumes. The same thing keeps happening. One man will get cornered, beg for mercy, receive mercy, and shoot the mercy-giver. After awhile they are both bleeding profusely and too injured to walk or yell anymore. The chase continues at a slow crawl until one of the men collapses and dies. Bereft, the other man turns his gun on himself, but he can't finagle the trigger.]*

SCENE 13
Starke, Therapist, Medical Students
Seminar XXVIII.

[On the floor of a surgical amphitheater, Starke sits across from the therapist whose voice we heard offstage in SCENE 5. *Scores of medical students watch them expectantly from the seating tiers that surround them.]*

THERAPIST [*in medias res*]: Resign yourself to bleakness.

STARKE [*in an Irish accent*]: I do. Of course I do. If nothing else, I'm self-aware, and I'm not afraid to admit it. I accept the bleakness of the state of my character. The problem is I get to feeling really bleak sometimes.

THERAPIST: Are you Irish?

STARKE [*in an Irish accent*]: No.

THERAPIST: Why are you speaking in an Irish accent? A bad one, I might add.

STARKE [*in an Irish accent*]: This is how I talk. I've always talked this way.

THERAPIST: This is the first time I have ever heard you talk that way. How unusual.

STARKE [*in an Irish accent*]: Say more.

THERAPIST: I think I've said quite enough.

[*Starke throws a temper tantrum and hurls his chair at the therapist. It misses. Starke retrieves the chair and hurls it into the amphitheater. It takes out several students. Starke runs in a furious circle until he tires out. Legs crossed, the therapist observes the tantrum idly, tapping his teeth with a pen.*]

STARKE [*dropping the Irish accent*]: I'm out of shape. When I was an infant, I could go on forever.

THERAPIST: Nothing is forever. Nothing except that which is beyond language and unassimilable to symbolization.

[*Starke throws another tantrum, but it doesn't last long. Piqued by an unforeseen memory, he begins to cry.*]

THERAPIST: I know. Life is hard. Existence is harder. [*Pauses.*] Narrative is the worst.

[*The students clap politely.*]

STARKE [*to the students*]: That's quite enough, gentlemen. I'm interested in the exploration of domestic time and space. [*To the therapist.*] You're notions of life, existence and narrative are neither here nor there. The exfoliation of my ego is the only issue under discussion today.

THERAPIST: And the homunculus?

[*The students snigger.*]

STARKE: What?

THERAPIST: The homunculus. You mentioned a homunculus.

[*Sniggering.*]

STARKE: A homunculus? I didn't mention any goddamn homunculus. [*Pauses.*] What's a homunculus? I don't know what that is.

[*Screaming, a homunculus falls from the heavens of the theater onto the stage. It lands between Starke and the therapist and explodes into plasma. The medical students cry out with joy.*]

STARKE [*exasperated*]: You realize I have a hangover, right? I was coaxed here with the promise of a mimosa. That's all that matters to me.

THERAPIST: Alcohol may lead to liver damage. Liver damage may cause death.

[*The students break out into an Irish drinking song . . .*]

[*Starke blitzes the therapist. The therapist tumbles forward out of his chair and plunges through a trap door. The students fall silent. Starke inspects the floor and tests the trap door with his shoe.*]

STARKE [*to the students*]: I think I hear somebody down there. Can anybody hear it?

[*The students use acoustic fans and ear trumpets for assistance. Starke kneels and puts his ear to the stage.*]

STARKE: You don't hear that? None of you? I hear something . . .

[*The students put away their instruments and quietly file out of the amphitheater as Starke descends into a trap door to confront the source of the commotion.*]

SCENE 14
Starke, Nathanial Hörnblowér
Purgatory.

[*Starke stands in one corner of the stage. In the opposite corner stands Nathaniel Hörnblowér, a stumpy man whose lower body tapers into a withered, semi-shrunken head. He wears a disheveled suit with rumpled coattails. Between them, center stage, is an old, industrial-sized copy machine. It looks like an antique Victrola.*]

STARKE [*shielding his eyes*]: Nathaniel? Is that you?

[*No response. Starke adjusts his tie and walks towards Nathaniel Hörnblowér, who, the moment Starke takes his first step, produces a corny mock-trumpet sound, blowing into the thumb of a hang-loose sign that he makes with his fingers.*]

[*Starke stops in his tracks. Nathaniel Hörnblowér stops trumpeting.*]

STARKE: Nathaniel? Nathanial Hörnblowér?

[*No response. Starke paces forward and Nathaniel Hörnblowér blows the faux coronet. Starke stops. Nathaniel Hörnblowér stops. They start and stop again. They do it again. Every time he moves his feet, Nathaniel Hörnblowér plays an inane tune, as if Starke is a clown-king entering a ballroom. Aggravated, he locks his knees and glares at Nathaniel Hörnblowér.*]

STARKE [*signaling the copy machine*]: What does that mean? Does it mean something? Should I attempt to process the apparatus with a nimble hermeneutic? I don't know what the apparatus is. But I can suck meaning from a sun-dried grassblade.

[*No response.*]

STARKE: Are we related by blood? Are you somebody? More to the point, are you my Uncle Nathanial Hörnblowér? Do you know Judge Bun, the elephant killer? Everybody thinks he's my son. But he's my father and I'm going to kill him.

[*No response.*]

STARKE: I'm going to mind my own business now. I hope you'll do the same.

[*He walks towards the copy machine and Nathaniel Hörnblowér blows the faux coronet. Starke doesn't stop. Surprised, Nathaniel Hörnblowér blows louder, faster. Starke proceeds forward. Nathaniel Hörnblowér works himself into a frenzy; soon his purple lips are spitting out a mangled version of "Flight of the Bumblebee."*]

[*When Starke reaches the copy machine, Nathaniel Hörnblowér doubles over and gasps for air, hands gripping his knees. Starke inspects the machine.*]

STARKE: There aren't any buttons or levers. I don't know what to do.

[*The machine comes to life and yields a copy on a sheet of paper. Starke retrieves the copy and studies it, pausing to glance around the theater, as if somebody is watching him, or a sniper has him in his sights. He doesn't say anything, although he clearly wants to speak. He's afraid for his life. The copy begins to shake in his pinched fingers. He's petrified and can't move.*]

[*Regaining his composure, Nathaniel Hörnblowér toots a friendly, off-key song, then takes a step backwards and jumps off the edge of the stage. The song dopplers into the Abyss.*]

SCENE 15
Starke, Deconstructionists, Giant Elephant Corpse
The stage of Forever.

[*A dead elephant lying on its side occupies the greater part of the stage. It's much bigger than the elephant that was tried and hung earlier in the play. Starke circles the corpse several times, gesticulating and talking to himself. He doesn't appear to notice it.*]

STARKE [*pausing*]: This reminds me of the stage of Forever. [*He stomps adamantly.*] I'm sick of not being able to punch people in my dreams! I think it's a result of not punching enough people in reality. The least I could do is punch a punching bag once a week. I'm a failure.

THERAPIST [*offstage*]: Why is it that you can't punch people in your dreams?

STARKE: I don't know. It's not that I don't try. The best I can do is strangle people in a lighthearted way. They think I'm trying to tickle them and make fun of me.

[*The therapist giggles as if somebody is tickling him. Starke begins to shadowbox, throwing wild and awkward punches; he can't even seem to land a punch on the face of thin air. Frustrated, he screams uncontrollably.*]

[*A legion of deconstructionists emerge from the trap doors. They all speak French and look French: skinny, rakish, tight suits, white bouffant hairdos, turtlenecks, wine-stained lips, superstylized beards, etc. They swear and shout at one another, quoting philosophers and theorists as they pace around and across the elephant, which, like Starke, escapes their attention. Starke observes the spectacle of contention agitatedly.*]

[*The elephant moans and rolls over, squashing a handful of deconstructionists. Their colleagues scream like wraiths, dash to the corners of the stage, throw themselves off and doppler into the Abyss.*]

[*Tentatively Starke inspects the elephant to see if it's still alive. He picks up a cane left behind by one of the deconstructionists and strikes the elephant repeatedly. It doesn't move.*]

STARKE [*hurling the cane offstage*]: Reality wins again! [*To the elephant.*] Good riddance you son of a bitch. [*Pauses.*] Good lord I miss my family. [*Kneels and prays.*] Dear lord, please exorcize all of the sons of bitches from my life and give me the strength and guilt-free dynamism to kill anybody I want to without getting caught by the Law of the Real. Amen.

SCENE 16
Starke, Mrs. Starke, Flang, Flang's Girlfriend, Judge Bun
Grandfather's pole barn.

[*A ladder angles up to a loft where Judge Bun lies with his arms dangling over the edge. He's wearing a black robe and his eyes gleam like chips of porcelain. Everybody else lingers beneath him.*]

STARKE: I hate it out here in grandpa's pole barn! It's dirtier than the attic. I hope that son of a bitch is in Hell!

MRS. STARKE: You don't believe in Hell, Mr. Starke.

STARKE: I believe in everything, by God! Stop calling me mister, Mrs. Starke.

[*Flang is making out with his girlfriend atop a tractor. She's the spitting image of Betty Boop: large eyes, short-cropped black hair, skimpy red flapper dress, etc. Flang's bedraggled suit has come undone. He makes loud chirping and sucking noises and his girlfriend moans like a kewpie doll.*]

STARKE· [*eyeballing Flang*]: It's one thing to fornicate in public. It's another thing to make noise while you're doing it. Life isn't a porno. This is grandpa's pole barn!

FLANG [*pausing*]: Fornicate? We're not fornicating. [*Flang's girlfriend titters.*] Do you even know what fornication is?

[*Starke eyeballs Mrs. Starke. He blushes and tries to shout something. Fails.*]

FLANG [*massaging his girlfriend's breasts*]: You big galoot. Have ever even taken your pants off? Let alone put them on.

STARKE: That's it! I've had enough of your jungle fury! [*He charges the tractor.*]

MRS. STARKE: Stop it, you two! Look! Judge Bun's arm is going to come loose again! Oh no!

STARKE [*still charging*]: Let it come loose! Nobody cares!

MRS. STARKE: You're a dirty monster, my sweet and beautiful husband! You poor man!

[*Both of Judge Bun's arms fall off and land on the stage. Like two ceramic vases, they explode into shards and dust, and a trap door claims Starke.*]

FLANG [*to Judge Bun*]: Prost! Zum Wohl! [*He kisses his girlfriend madly and climbs onto her.*]

[*Hysterical, Mrs. Starke sifts through the ashes of Judge Bun's arms, then steps on the ladder and lumbers up it, awkwardly, one rung at a time, mumbling about how frightened she is . . . Near the top she loses her balance. Arms waving, she falls backwards onto the stage and plunges through a trapdoor.*]

SCENE 17
Starke, Flang, Dentist, Dental Assistant, Henchmen
Dentist's office.

[*Reclined in a dental chair, Starke holds a gun to a dentist's head while the trembling dentist searches his mouth with a mirror and a pick. Three henchman in overalls stand nearby. When he's not talking, Starke holds his mouth open.*]

STARKE [*to the dentist*]: If you tell me I have a cavity, you're dead.

FLANG: Shoot the dirty son of a bitch! Shoot him!

DENTIST: Please don't shoot me.

STARKE: I'll do as I please! [*To Flang.*] Plug your hole!

DENTAL ASSISTANT: I think I see a cavity.

DENTIST [*to the dental assistant*]: Please don't say that.

STARKE [*pointing the gun at the dental assistant*]: What did you say? Say that again.

FLANG: Shoot her! Shoot her!

STARKE: Flang! By god, holster that drama!

DENTIST: She said she thinks she sees an anomaly. But I think she meant to say she sees a . . . a calamity. No, I mean a . . . a . . . a happily. That's what she said she sees, I mean.

STARKE [*cocking the gun*]: She sees a *happily* in my mouth? That goddamn nonsensical. That's a goddamn adverb with nothing to modify.

DENTIST: Is that what I said? I don't remember. It frightens me when patients point guns at me.

DENTAL ASSISTANT: I said I see a *cavity*. You know what I said! It's right there! Look!

HENCHMAN #1 [*leaning towards Starke*]: She's right. I see it.

HENCHMAN #2: I see it, too.

HENCHMAN #3: There it is.

STARKE [*pointing the gun at the henchmen*]: My ass. Who the hell are you rednecks anyway?

[*The henchmen trade perplexed glances.*]

HENCHMAN #1: You hired us. We're here to protect you. We belong to you.

STARKE: Nobody belongs to me. I don't even belong to me. I belong to my Old Lady. That's all I know.

HENCHMAN #2: You hired us to protect you from Mrs. Starke.

STARKE: That's ridiculous. She's an angel. She's a good woman. She's the reason I get up in the morning. [*Pauses.*] Why would that old bitch want to do anything to me? I didn't do anything to her. I've never done anything to anyone.

HENCHMAN #3: You told us she hired Judge Bun to kill you.

STARKE: *Hired* Judge Bun? He's a mollusk! He can't walk. He can't even keep his arms on! And it's King Bun.

FLANG: They're telling the truth.

STARKE: Nobody tells the truth, my son. The nature of language prohibits it. Symbolization and signification are the best we can do. Wise up.

HENCHMAN #1: If you say so.

STARKE: You're goddamn right I say so. Mrs. Starke may be after me but those outfits are impossible. Who dressed you weirdos this morning, you're dead grandmother? My grandma's dead but she'd never put me in that racket. The least you could have done is take some initiative and yank on cheap suits. Fine. You say you belong to me. If you belong to me, I can tell you what to do. Run away. That's what I want you to do. Run away like three blind mice. Do it.

[*Nobody moves. Starke points the gun overhead and fires off several rounds. The henchmen make a break for it. Starke lowers the gun and shoots them as they flee, expending all of his bullets. He hits them as they reach the edge of the stage and topple over. Moaning in pain, the henchmen doppler into the Abyss.*]

[*Starke unloads the empty clip and slams in a new one.*]

STARKE [*putting the gun back on the dental assistant*]: What's that you said about a cavity?

DENTAL ASSISTANT: You are a bad man.

STARKE: Am I? Be careful, then. Bad men do bad things.

DENTAL ASSISTANT: I'm not afraid of you. I said you have a cavity. A disgusting-looking cavity. I could see that thing from miles away. It's horrible! I couldn't get that monstrosity out with a pick-axe. You're grotesque! I—"

[*Starke shoots her in the face. Her head explodes, leaving nothing. Blood spurts from the neckhole as the dental assistant staggers backwards and gropes at the air. She falls into a trap door.*]

[*The dentist shrieks, faints. Flang leaps onto him and clubs him in the head with his forearms. Starke jumps out of the chair and kicks Flang off of the dentist. Flang slides across the stage and nearly falls off. At the edge, he does a skillful somersault and hops onto his feet. Starke kneels and checks the pulse of the dentist.*]

STARKE [*incensed*]: He's dead! You hairy idiot! Who's going to clean my teeth now?

[*Starke dashes towards Flang and tries to tackle him. Hooting, Flang leaps onto the underside of a passing gondola that ferries him away.*]

STARKE [*to himself*]: Atta boy, Flang. . . . Keep your eye on the sun and ignore the moonbeams.

[*Laying on his chest, Starke watches Flang go. A trap door opens on the other side of the stage. Starke screams and thrashes his limbs as he is sucked across the stage into it.*]

SCENE 18
Starke
Nowhere.

[*As in the beginning of* SCENE 5, *Starke crawls in and out of trap doors and scuttles around the stage on all fours. Per usual, he wears a three-piece suit.*]

SCENE 19
Starke
Nowhere.

[*Repeat* SCENE 18, *only now Starke is naked and pauses occasionally to clean his nostrils and chew on his fingernails and toenails. At one point he cries out.*]

SCENE 20
STARKE
Nowhere.

[*A trap door spits out Starke like a pinch of tobacco. He's still naked. He gets up and stomps on the trap door. He does a monkey dance and makes a spectacle of himself.*]

STARKE: You son of a bitch! I'm still alive you ugly bastard! I'll kill you!

[*He stomps on the trap door until he sprains an ankle and falls backwards into another trap door.*]

SCENE 20
Starke, Mrs. Starke
Grandmother's boudoir.

[*A half-square of lavender silk curtains define the contours of a boudoir situated in a stage corner. In the middle is an ornate Victorian canopy bed where Mrs. Starke lies passed out in an unlaced corset and frilled underwear. To one side is a vanity table; in place of a mirror is a television screen on which random clips from Hitchcock movies run backwards.*]

[*An armoire stands on the other side of the bed. There is a commotion inside, then the doors swing open and Starke steps out wearing slippers and a velour smoking jacket. He holds an oversized martini glass.*]

STARKE [*peering around the room*]: Holy christ I've never been in grandma's boudoir before. It's clean! And yet I feel dirty. [*He takes a sip of the martini.*] Holy hell that tastes good! I've been hung over for years. Now the hangover's gone. One sip of goodness is all it took. Surely another sip will only improve my life. [*He takes another sip.*] I feel the same.

[*Mrs. Starke groans from the bed.*]

STARKE: Ah! There you are Mrs. Starke. I've been looking all over for you. Why did you run out of the party like that? Your Cinderella complex is finally getting the better of you.

[*Mrs. Starke groans from the bed.*]

STARKE: Mrs. Starke? Mrs. Starke? Mrs. Starke? Are you all right? [*He takes another sip.*] I still feel the same. The same will have to do.

[*Mrs. Starke groans louder.*]

STARKE: Jesus what should I do? Should I call the doctor? Who is our doctor? Do we have one? Well what should I do? Should I do something? [*Sips.*]

[*Belching, Mrs. Starke rolls off the bed, slams onto the stage, cries out, and rolls under the bed. Starke finishes his martini as he skips not-so-quickly to her aid. He tosses the glass aside and looks under the bed. He gets up and goes to the other side of the bed and looks under it. He gets up and lifts the mattress and looks under it. He looks under the bed one more time and shoots to his feet.*]

STARKE: She's gone!

SCENE 21
Starke, Mrs. Starke
Grandmother's boudoir.

[*Same setting as* SCENE 20. *Starke steps out of the armoire with a martini.*]

STARKE [*peering around the room*]: Holy christ I've never been in grandma's boudoir before. It's clean! And yet I feel dirty. [*He takes a sip of the martini.*] Holy hell that tastes good! I've been hung over for years. Now the hangover's gone. One sip of goodness is all it took. Surely another sip will only improve my life.

[*He takes another sip.*] I feel the same.

[*Mrs. Starke groans from the bed.*]

STARKE: Ah! There you are Mrs. Starke. I've been looking all over for you. Why did you run out of the party like that? Your Cinderella complex is finally getting the better of you.

[*Mrs. Starke leaps off of the bed and grapples onto Starke like a rabid animal. She screams over and over and won't let go.*]

STARKE: Mrs. Starke? Mrs. Starke? Mrs. Starke? Are you all right? [*Staggering around the boudoir, he tries to take another sip of the martini, but Mrs. Starke knocks away the glass.*] I still feel the same! The same will have to do!

[*He throws an elbow and catches Mrs. Starke on the chin. She loosens her grasp and melts to the floor. Starke backs away.*]

STARKE [*glaring at Mrs. Starke*]: Jesus what should I do? Should I call the doctor? Who is our doctor? Do we have one? Well what should I do? Should I do something? [*Chews fingernail.*]

[*Frothing at the mouth, Mrs. Starke growls and barks, then falls forward onto her chest and rolls under the bed. Starke picks up the martini glass and laps at the residue of alcohol in the cone. He tosses the glass aside and looks under the bed. He gets up and goes to the other side of the bed and looks under it. He gets up and lifts the mattress and looks under it. He looks under the bed one more time and shoots to his feet.*]

STARKE: She's gone!

SCENE 22
Starke
Grandmother's boudoir.

[*Same setting as* SCENE 20 *and* 21, *only there's no sign of Mrs. Starke. Starke steps out of the armoire with a martini.*]

STARKE [*peering around the room*]: Holy christ I've never been in grandma's boudoir before. It's clean! And yet I feel dirty. [*He takes a sip of the martini.*] Holy hell that tastes good! I've been hung over for years. Now the hangover's gone. One sip of goodness is all it took. Surely another sip will only improve my life. [*He takes another sip.*] I feel the same.

[*Starke realizes the bed is empty.*]

STARKE: She's gone!

SCENE 23
Starke
Grandmother's boudoir.

[*Same setting as* SCENE 20-22. *Starke steps out of the armoire with a martini.*]

STARKE [*peering around the room*]: Holy christ I've never been in grandma's boudoir before. It's clean! And yet I feel dirty. [*He takes a sip of the martini.*] Holy hell that's water! I've been cornholed by the bartender! [*He takes another sip.*] I feel the same.

[*Starke realizes the bed is empty.*]

STARKE: She's gone.

SCENE 24
Starke
Grandmother's boudoir.

[*Same setting as* SCENE 20-23.]

STARKE [*locked in the armoire*]: She's gone! She's gone! She's gone! She's gone! She's gone!

SCENE 25
Elephant
Somewhere.

[*An elephant stands center stage. Occasionally it yawns and swipes flies from its hide with its tail. Otherwise it doesn't move.*]

SCENE 26
Starke, Flang, Bun
A clearing.

[*Bun stands in the middle of a broken firepit. He is frail and withered, but he maintains a powerful stance. His white eyes bulge menacingly from the stalk of a desiccated head. Nearby Flang crouches in ostensible fear. Starke circles the firepit like a predator.*]

STARKE: Whore!

FLANG: Don't call him that!

STARKE: I was talking about Mrs. Starke, not Judge Bun. God bless her soul.

FLANG: King Bun.

BUN [*voice like an electric reed*]: I am neither Judge nor King. I am only Bun.

[*Flang screams.*]

STARKE: Man up, Flang. Now's not the time to lose your Dog. [*To Bun.*] Call yourself whatever you want. Either way you're still a killer. That elephant was an innocent slave. You sentenced it to oblivion.

BUN: There is no oblivion. There is only the Dark Hypotenuse. [*Pauses.*] There is only . . . Starke. And Starke-ness. [*Flang explodes like a piñata.*] Goodbye father. I love you.

[*A bouquet of white flames erupts from the firepit and incinerates Bun.*]

SCENE 25
Fleeting-Improvised Man
The museum of dead curtains.

[*Live-action rendition of Francis Bacon's "Study after Velazquez's Portrait of Pope Innocent X." Center stage, a flickering, screaming man dressed like a pope sits in a gold throne, the arms of which he grips tightly, as if he's on a rollercoaster to Hell. He wears a white robe, round spectacles, purple pellegrina and mitre. His wide-open mouth is too big for his head. His bleached white teeth fluoresce as he screams in agony. The scream is endless. He never takes a breath.*]

SCENE 26
Homunculus
The surface.

[*At a snail's pace, an armless homunculus crawls out of a trap door, worms across the stage and over the edge. It doesn't make a sound.*]

SCENE 27
Eternity.

[*Empty stage. A full minute passes and then a trap door falls open. The squeak of the swinging door echoes throughout the theater as the audience slows to a halt.*]

CURTAIN

PRIMACY

CHARACTERS

Man
Woman

The clamor of machinery surges . . . and dies. A man crawls halfway across the stage and collapses onto his stomach. A woman enters and slowly ambles towards him, feeling her way, as if she's in a dark closet and can't see anything. Eventually she steps on the man and shrieks, waking him.

WOMAN

Is that you! Is that you!

MAN

Stands.

No.

Pause.

I mean yes, it's me. I'm here.

WOMAN

Oh.

MAN

Where are we?

WOMAN

I don't know.

Pause.

The back yard?

MAN

That makes sense. I must have been sleepcrawling again. Whenever I sleepcrawl, I end up in the back yard.

Pause.

Forgive me.

WOMAN

It's not a sin to sleepcrawl into the back yard.

MAN

No?

Pause.

If that's not a sin, I don't know what is.

WOMAN

Fearfully.

Are you sure you're all right?

MAN

Looks down at himself.

I'm fine. I think I'm fine. Why would you ask me something like that?

WOMAN

Well, you know.

Pause.

This morning on the bus you had a knife in your mouth.

Pause.

Remember?

MAN

Long pause.

A knife?

Long pause.

A knife?

Long pause.

No I did not!

WOMAN

I was so frightened.

Pause.

Everybody was looking at you.

Pause.

After awhile you threw the knife out the window and we got off at the next stop. You dragged me to that diner, shouted at the cashier, and the police arrested you on the sidewalk, burger in hand.

Pause.

Remember the warrant?

MAN

Long pause.

Warrant?

Long pause.

Burger?

Long pause.

That never happened!

WOMAN

Sobs.

But it DID happen! It did!

Long pause.

Maybe it didn't.

Pause.

Well. You're probably just hung over.

Pause.

Bad things happen when you're hung over.

Pause.

Your hangovers bring reality to its knees.

MAN

Long pause.

Hangover?

Long pause.

Hangover?

Long pause.

Hangover?

Long pause.

I haven't had a drink in hours!

Faints.

WOMAN

Oh my goodness!

Kicks the man in the ribs.

Are you all right?

Kicks the man in the ribs.

Are you all right?

Kicks the man in the ribs.

Don't leave me here! I'm afraid of the back yard!

Flurry of kicks to the ribs.

MAN

Awakens.

There's nothing to be afraid of.

Tries to stand.

Ak!

Falls down. Gets up, clutching his ribcage.

Back yards are harmless. They can't hurt you. Back yards are like children: they get on your nerves; they reduce you to raw indignation; they repeat themselves like possessed demons, blathering on and on, if only by way of the unspeakable grass—every time you cut it, it grows back again, and then you cut it and it grows back again, and again, relentlessly; sometimes they scream and keep you up all night . . . but the fact is you love them. You love the back yards for what they are and what you don't want them to be.

Contorting in pain.

Ak!

Falls to his knees.

WOMAN

Are you all right?

Pause.

What's wrong?

MAN

Nothing. I'll be all right. Bad dream.

Pause.

Bad dreams smart when you wake up.

Pause.

Morning is the worst. Morning is the elbow of vulnerability.

Pause.

That reminds me. I need to revise my obituary at once. The first draft was a piece of hackwork.

Pause.

Get a pen and paper.

Pause.

Scratch that. Just memorize what I tell you. I'll dictate the revision. I know it by rote.

WOMAN

All right.

Concentrates.

I'm ready.

MAN

Good.

Pause.

FYI there will be a lot of action scenes in this obit. It'll be less like a lecture on organizational leadership and more like a kung fu movie, with lots of flying kicks and bloodspatter. There will be no advice or information at all regarding how to be an efficient and effective manager, landlord or superintendent. Ok?

WOMAN

Ok.

Concentrates. Balks. Concentrates again.

I'm ready.

MAN

You already said you're ready. Now then.

Long pause.

How do obituaries start again? I forgot. They all start the same way, don't they? There's a formula.

WOMAN

I think they begin with names and places. So-and-so, a resident of somewhere-or-other . . . Like that.

Pause.

Then you mention that the person died. In this case, you.

Pause.

But you're not dead.

MAN

I know.

Pause.

I know that!

Pause.

No guff from the peanut gallery. Just memorize what I say.

WOMAN

All right.

Shrieks.

MAN

What's wrong with you!

WOMAN

I'm worried that I won't be able to memorize your obituary word for word.

Pause.

Is my memory allowed to paraphrase?

MAN

No paraphrasing. Verbatim—or nothing.

WOMAN

All right.

Shrieks.

MAN

Stop that!

Pause.

The best obituaries are composed in the darkest silences.

Pause.

Now then.

Pause.

So-and-so, a resident of something-or-other . . .

WOMAN

No. You're supposed to say your name. Your own name. And where you live . . .

MAN

I'm just warming up!

Pause.

Isn't a man allowed to warm up?

Pause.

If I were lifting weights and I didn't stretch, I'd pull all of my muscles. The same goes for writing obituaries.

WOMAN

You don't lift weights. Why would you lift weights?

MAN

I don't know. It's a hypothesis.

Pause.

No. That's the wrong word.

Pause.

It's a scenario.

Pause.

Well, yes. But no. It's not just a scenario. It's much more than a scenario.

Pause.

It's a hypothetical scenario.

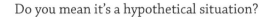

WOMAN

Do you mean it's a hypothetical situation?

MAN

What's the difference between a scenario and a situation?

Pause.

No more questions!

Falls over.

WOMAN

Oh dear!

MAN

I'm all right.

Pause.

I fell.

Pause.

I may have fainted again.

Pause.

My ribs hurt.

Pause.

I'm all right.

WOMAN

Get up! Get up!

Shrieks.

MAN

Stands.

I'm up!

WOMAN

We've got to get out of here.

Pause.

This place is giving me the creeps.

MAN

It's just a back yard. Grass, a few bushes, and an outhouse. There's nothing more innocuous. It's the safest place in the world.

WOMAN

The grass is lime green—it's teeming with fertilizer and pollutants and toxins. The bushes contain all manner of

thorns and poisonous berries. Beneath the outhouse is a pit
of stinking fecal matter.

Pause.

This back yard is a death trap!

MAN

The abject can't kill you.

Pause

The poison in those berries can't kill you.

Pause.

If you don't throw yourself into the bushes, the thorns can't
prick you.

Pause.

The toxins in the grass might give you psoriasis, but there's
ointment for that.

Long pause.

All is well.

WOMAN

Prays.

MAN

Stop praying! God doesn't care if you get a skin rash.

WOMAN

Scratching herself.

It itches!

Shrieks.

MAN

You're faking it! You're faking it!

WOMAN

Stops scratching herself.

Maybe it doesn't itch.

MAN

You're goddamn right it doesn't itch. Stop demonizing the back yard!

Sound of a baby crying offstage.

What's that?

WOMAN

The baby. You woke it.

MAN

Baby?

WOMAN

Our baby is crying.

Listens.

Yes. That's our baby.

MAN

What baby?

Pause.

We don't have a baby.

WOMAN

We don't?

Listens.

The baby stops crying.

Oh.

MAN

Right. I think I'll begin my obituary *in medias res*. Like *Oedipus the King*. Like *Raging Bull*. Like any good narrative.

WOMAN

All right.

Pause.

But don't strain yourself too much. At lunch you could barely lift the soup spoon to your mouth. You were so jaundiced and withered after you drank that arsenic.

MAN

If my prescriptions were filled on time, I wouldn't have to self-medicate!

Pause.

I thought it was a cup of chamomile tea.

Pause.

It's not like I'm scaling a cliff. I'm not going to throw my back out writing my obituary.

Long pause.

So there I am, a joystick in the dirt . . .

WOMAN

Sobs.

That's not *in medias res*. That's *sub finem*! *Jesu Juva*!

Pause.

They don't talk about burying bodies in obituaries.

MAN

They do in mine! My obituary can be anything I want it to be and I can assure you a lot happens after they bury me. There's a big, like, battle royal at the cemetery with priests and popes and all kinds of holy men flying over the gravestones on wires in a terrific wuxia death match.

Pause.

I haven't decided what prompts the death match yet. Surely idle grief isn't a viable catalyst.

WOMAN

Attacks the man.

I'll kill you if you die! I'll kill you if you die!

MAN

Falls down.

Stop it! You'll wake the baby!

WOMAN

Shh!

Listens.

I don't hear anything.

Listens.

I still don't hear anything.

MAN

I'm sure everything is fine.

WOMAN

Kicks the man in the ribs.

Everything is fine! Everything is fine!

Kicks the man in the head.

MAN

Ak!

Passes out.

The clamor of machinery comes to life. The woman looks over her shoulder and pensively wanders offstage. The man rolls over several times. Eventually he pushes himself to hands and knees and begins to crawl towards the audience, head dangling like a dead limb. He collapses on the apron of the stage. Upstage, a giant enters, lopes from one side to the other, and exits. The man stirs and mumbles to himself. He cries out. He calls for help. The woman enters, running . . . She trips, falls down, slides across the stage on her stomach, lies still, gets up and limps the rest of the way.

WOMAN

Wake up.

Kicks the man in the ribs with her hurt leg.

Ak!

Kicks the man in the ribs with her good leg. Loses balance and falls over.

Ak!

MAN

Ak!

Awakens.

I had a bad dream.

Lifts head.

I dreamt I was at a train station in Milan. I was pretending to be a British expatriate again, speaking in that faux Cockney accent to a cabal of English tourists. I honestly believed they thought I had been born and raised in the East End, then moved to Canada as an adolescent.

Pause.

That was the bad part. My confidence in their perception of me as the genuine article.

Pause.

Then again, it's only bad in retrospect. In the dream, I didn't know that they knew I was faking it. Only now, here, drunk on consciousness, do I recognize their awareness of my raw fraudulence. Hence it was a good dream.

Pause.

Or just a dream. There was nothing particularly good about it.

Long pause.

I have a headache.

WOMAN

Of course you do. Don't you remember how much you drank at the salon? You mixed your drinks, too—beer, wine, champagne, at least four martinis, then all those shots of Southern Comfort.

Pause.

Again and again you threw yourself down the stairway! You said you could do it better than Dali.

Pause.

"I have no reason for doing this!" you yelled.

Pause.

Nobody believed you. So you kept doing it.

Pause.

Remember?

MAN

Long pause.

No I did not!

WOMAN

Then you attacked that poor rector.

Pause.

He wasn't expecting to be blindsided by you.

Sobs.

I felt so badly for him!

Sobs.

But not as badly as I felt for the paramedics.

Sniffles.

You nearly killed them.

Sniffles.

Remember the way their eyes fell into their skulls?

MAN

Long pause.

No they did not!

WOMAN

I don't know what to do with you sometimes. One moment you're a horrible drunk, the next you're a perfect gentleman.

Pause.

I'd rather you were a drunk all the time. Then I'd know what to expect.

Pause.

But you have this determination to be sober. Nobody likes you sober. You and sobriety are a bad mix. Like water and dirt. That makes mud.

Pause.

I'm glad you're not a gentleman all the time. Nobody likes a fulltime goody-goody.

Pause.

You haven't asked me out on a date in years.

MAN

A date?

Pause.

Are you calling me mud?

Pause.

I am so much more than mud. I have feelings. I have desires. Last night I dreamt that I saved bonobos from extinction, and I didn't even have a Rambo knife. Is that what a greasy piece of mud would do?

Long pause.

Bonobos are good people. Everybody knows it.

Pause.

But I'm trying to write my obituary. There's no time for love and war.

Passes out.

WOMAN

There's always time for the little things in life.

Pause.

That's your problem. You never make any time for the little things.

Pause.

I hate the back yard. I don't care if it's innocuous.

Long pause.

The only things that matter are my feelings.

The woman bends over and takes the man by the ankles. Limping, she drags him upstage, turns and drags him offstage. Silence. Soon the man crawls back onstage and collapses onto his stomach. The woman enters maneuvering a crutch. She lumbers towards the man and accidentally stabs him in the groin with the tip.

MAN

Ak!

WOMAN

Is that you! Is that you!

MAN

Clutching himself.

No.

Pause.

I mean yes.

Pause.

No. I mean no, I think.

Moans.

WOMAN

Where are we?

MAN

I know this place.

Pause.

It's the front yard.

WOMAN

Everybody's staring at us. All of our neighbors.

MAN

The front yard isn't like the back yard.

Pause.

There's no privacy.

WOMAN

I don't like it.

MAN

Looks backstage.

Maybe we should go in the house.

WOMAN

I've been in the house before.

Pause.

There's nothing to do in there.

MAN

Stands.

All of my bones feel like they're broken. I'm going to sit on the grass.

Sits.

That feels better.

Pause.

How did we get here?

WOMAN

You were sleepcrawling again.

Pause.

I followed you around for awhile, then lost you in the sun.

MAN

Sleepcrawling?

Pause.

That's ridiculous.

Pause.

Who crawls around in their sleep?

Pause.

Nobody.

Pause.

People walk in their sleep. They don't crawl.

WOMAN

Fine. Then you were crawling around on the earth of your own free, conscious will.

MAN

Long pause.

Maybe I was sleepcrawling after all.

WOMAN

To the audience.

What are you looking at!

Hyperventilates.

Ak!

To the audience.

You've never seen a man sitting in the grass before?

Shrieks.

We're not doing anything wrong!

To the man.

The neighbors won't stop looking at us.

To the audience.

Stop looking at us!

MAN

Since when do we have neighbors?

Looks backstage.

I don't see anybody.

Looks at the audience.

There's nobody out there.

Pause.

Neighbors are a fiction. The only reality is the inside of your own head.

WOMAN

The front yard is the only reality, if you ask me. This is far worse than the back yard. It's embarrassing.

Pause.

I'd rather be frightened than embarrassed.

MAN

When I'm finished writing my obituary, please bury me in the front yard.

Pause.

Stick a tombstone over me that reads: HEREIN LIES THE GNARLED BONES OF TRUTH.

Long pause.

You'll have to re-plant after you dig the grave, put me in it and cover me with dirt, but if you get good hydroseed, the grass will grow back greener than before.

Pause.

Get the tombstone at the grocery store. They sell them real cheap. Or you could just stick a fork in there. In the dirt, I mean. I like forks.

WOMAN

I don't want the grass to grow back greener than before.

Pause.

Then there'll be a big green rectangle on the lawn. Everybody will see it.

Shrieks.

MAN

Ok fine.

Pause.

Don't reseed the grave. Buy a patch of sod and match the color.

Pause.

Mind you, sod is a lot more expensive than hydroseed.

Pause.

Don't worry about any of that right now. I haven't finished my obituary yet.

WOMAN

You have. You have finished a first draft and moved on to the revision process. You said so.

Pause.

You said you had already written a revision and committed it to memory.

Pause.

You said you knew the revision by heart.

MAN

By rote.

WOMAN

What?

MAN

Who's writing this obituary?

Pause.

It's my obituary!

Pause.

When you write your obituary, you can do what you want.

Pause.

Stop trying to control me.

WOMAN

I'm not trying to control you. I'm saying what you said.

Pause.

What did you say?

MAN

I know what I said.

WOMAN

Do you?

Pause.

Last week at Thanksgiving dinner you said the same thing.

Pause.

You said, "I know what I said," after you reneged on your promise to everybody about the turkey.

Pause.

Do you remember your promise?

Pause.

You said you wanted to cook the turkey for Thanksgiving dinner. You said to invite everybody over.

Pause.

I invited everybody over.

Pause.

The children were so excited. They didn't eat for two days to build up an appetite.

Pause.

You cooked the turkey.

Pause.

You put it on the table.

Sobs.

You asked everybody to hold hands and said a long prayer, replacing God's name with your own.

Sobs.

After grace you sharpened the knife for awhile.

Sobs harder.

I could see the reflection of your crazy eyes flash in the knife when it passed by your face.

Shrieks.

Then you threw the knife aside and ate the whole turkey with your hands!

Shrieks.

Nobody could believe it.

Sniffles.

Everybody expected you to stop at some point and serve out portions.

Pause.

You didn't stop. You didn't serve out portions.

Pause.

You ate the turkey and then you ate the corn and the mashed potatoes too. And the pickles. All of them.

Pause.

The children were devastated.

Strikes the man with the crutch and falls over.

MAN

Ak!

WOMAN

Groping on the floor.

Remember?

MAN

Long pause.

It was my turkey!

WOMAN

Shrieks.

Stop it! You'll wake the dog!

MAN

Shh!

Listens.

I don't hear anything.

Listens.

I still don't hear anything.

WOMAN

I'm sure everything is fine.

Offstage a dog whimpers and dies.

Or unfine.

MAN

Lunges for the woman and falls over.

You killed the baby!

Groping on the floor.

Baby killer!

WOMAN

That wasn't the baby! That was the dog!

Shrieks.

I should go see if everything is unfine.

Pulls her body across stage as if her legs are dead.

I'll be back later.

Inches forward.

Actually I'm never coming back to the front yard.

Inches forward.

We've given the neighbors an eyeful. They deserve worse.

MAN

Pursues the woman, pulling his body across stage as if his legs are dead.

Come back here.

Inches forward.

We don't have neighbors. We're the only house on the block.

Inches forward.

Don't blame your killing spree on the front yard.

Grabs the woman's ankle.

Gotcha!

Shakes the ankle like a tambourine.

Stop trying to get away from me!

WOMAN

Kicks the man in the face with her hurt leg.

Ak!

MAN

Ak!

Passes out.

WOMAN

Inches forward.

Are you all right!

Inches forward.

Are you all right!

Inches forward.

I'll kill you if you die!

Shrieks.

What's that noise? I hear something in the kitchen.

Pulls herself offstage.

The lights darken. We hear the bluster of storm winds and ocean surf . . . then midnight silence. The lights come back on. The man lies downstage on his back. He's still unconscious.

WOMAN

Offstage.

Get your hands off of me! Don't touch me!

Rolls onstage, across the stage, and offstage, shrieking.

MAN

Awakens.

Ak!

Sits and stares.

That dream was pure ennui. It's not even worth going to sleep anymore these days.

Pause.

When I was an orphan, my nightmares were the only things that kept me company.

WOMAN

Offstage.

You're talking to yourself.

MAN

Glances over shoulders.

Who said that?

WOMAN

Help! Help!

MAN

Listens.

What's that noise?

Listens.

I hear something in the kitchen.

WOMAN

Ak!

MAN

Long pause.

I guess I didn't hear anything. Sometimes I don't hear things.

Pause.

Where am I?

WOMAN

The roof!

MAN

Looks around.

Roof? What roof?

WOMAN

The roof of our house! I fell off!

Shrieks.

Ak!

MAN

Cocks head.

The roof?

Pauses.

The roof?

Throws hands in air and somersaults sideways offstage.

There is a commotion like animals fighting in bushes and tumbling through underbrush. The stage is empty. It remains empty for the rest of the play.

MAN

Offstage.

Get your hands off me! Don't touch me!

WOMAN

Offstage.

I didn't touch you!

MAN

Ak!

WOMAN

Are you all right? Don't die!

MAN

Pause.

I'm alive. Only my soul is dead.

WOMAN

Sobs.

Your poor soul! Let's bury it.

Whimpers.

MAN

Wise up! Nobody buries their souls.

Pause.

Where are we?

WOMAN

Sniffles.

The back yard? I can't see anything.

MAN

It's not the back yard. I know what the backyard feels like.

Pause.

It's not the front yard either. I know what the front yard smells like.

Pause.

Is there something between the front and the back yard?

WOMAN

Long pause.

No.

MAN

Well we must be somewhere. We can't just be nowhere.

WOMAN

Tentatively.

Are we in our graves?

MAN

That's ridiculous.

Pause.

People don't fall off of roofs into graves.

Pause.

What's wrong with you?

WOMAN

Tentatively.

Why did you torture that mortician?

MAN

Pause.

Mortician?

WOMAN

Long pause.

Curt shriek.

MAN

What's wrong with you?

WOMAN

I thought I saw something.

MAN

We can't see anything. It's dark.

WOMAN

Tentatively.

You tortured the mortician!

Shrieks.

MAN

Ak!

WOMAN

You did!

Pause.

Remember?

MAN

Clears phlegm from throat and spits.

WOMAN

He was just a mortician!

Pause.

He didn't know what he did wrong. Nobody did.

Pause.

You repeated the phrase "extreme interrogation tactics" as you beat him.

Pause.

He didn't kill your parents!

Pause.

He didn't even bury them.

Pause.

He organized the burial and sold you the coffins.

Pause.

The mortician ran the mortuary. That's what morticians do.

Pause.

It was a nightmare. Then, at the cocktail party afterwards, you took that sledgehammer and—

MAN

Ak!

WOMAN

What's wrong?

MAN

I thought of how to end my obituary. Or begin it. Wherever you begin or end an obituary—it's the end.

WOMAN

I thought you were going to revise the whole thing?

Pause.

I mean, I thought you had memorized a revision of the document.

Pause.

I can't remember.

MAN

Memory is like ice vapor: the moment you inhale it is the moment you lose yourself.

WOMAN

Long pause.

I guess so. Can you inhale ice vapor?

Inhales deeply.

What is ice vapor?

MAN

Clears phlegm from throat and spits.

No, that's the end of my obituary.

Pause.

The final line.

Pause.

The line people will remember when they read my obituary.

Pause.

In a sense, that's my entire obituary.

Pause.

My life and my death.

Long pause.

The lizard of syntax that will scuttle into eternity.

Pause.

I'm going to publish it in *The Daily Trystero*.

Long pause.

I might publish it in *The Pain Dealer*, too.

Long pause.

Can you publish the same obituary in competing venues? I'm not sure.

Long pause.

Here is the research element of my project.

WOMAN

Long pause.

Shrieks.

Long pause.

I can't feel my legs.

MAN

Long pause.

They're beneath you.

WOMAN

Long pause.

Oh.

Yawns.

I'll kill you if you die.

MAN

I'm alive. I think I'm alive.

Pause.

Did you find your legs?

WOMAN

Long pause.

No.

Yawns.

I don't know.

Long pause.

I found this.

MAN

Long pause.

I don't know what this is.

Long pause.

I can't see anything.

Long pause.

I can't feel anything.

Long pause.

Except for my legs. They're beneath me.

Long pause.

I don't know where you are.

Long pause.

Where are you?

WOMAN

Long pause.

The baby.

Yawns.

I found the baby.

Yawns.

It's in my arms.

Pause.

With me.

Pause.

Here.

Long pause.

It's licking my ear.

Yawns.

It's cooing so softly.

Yawns.

It loves me.

Long pause.

It loves me.

Yawns.

It's in my arms.

Yawns.

It's in my arms.

Yawns.

Yawns.

Dies.

MAN

Long pause.

That's not the baby.

Long pause.

That's the dog.

Long pause.

I can smell it.

Long pause.

It smells like ice vapor.

Long pause.

Are you all right?

Long pause.

I can't hear you.

Long pause.

Ak!

Long pause.

Ak!

Long pause.

I fell.

Long pause.

I'm all right, though.

Long pause.

I'll be all right.

Long pause.

No revision is needed.

Long pause.

Everything is as it should be.

Long pause.

Unfine.

Long pause.

Perfectly unfine.

Long pause.

Like ice vapor.

Inhales deeply.

Like the retreat of a hangover into the cornstalks.

Inhales deeply.

I can barely remember how I got here.

Long pause.

I must have been sleepcrawling again.

Long pause.

Whenever I sleepcrawl, I end up somewhere.

Long pause.

Are you there?

Long pause.

Are you there?

Long pause.

Where did you go?

Long pause.

Can you feel your legs?

Long pause.

You're not talking.

Long pause.

You're not crying.

Long pause.

You're not shrieking.

Long pause.

You're not breathing.

Long pause.

Are you dead?

Long pause.

Are you dead?

Long pause.

Can you feel your legs?

Long pause.

Don't die.

Long pause.

Don't die.

Long pause.

Don't die.

Long pause.

Don't die.

Long pause.

I'll kill you if you die . . .

CURTAIN

THREE PLAYS

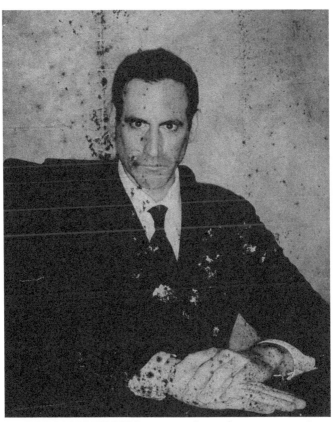

D. HARLAN WILSON is a novelist, short story writer, editor, literary critic, and Professor of English at Wright State University-Lake Campus. In addition to over twenty works of fiction and nonfiction, hundreds of his stories and essays have appeared in magazines, journals and anthologies throughout the world in multiple languages. Wilson serves as reviews editor for *Extrapolation*, editor-in-chief of Anti-Oedipus Press, and managing editor of Guide Dog Books. This is his first book of plays.

www.DHarlanWilson.com
www.TheKyotoMan.com